CHILD CUSTODY
SURVIVAL GUIDE

CHILD CUSTODY SURVIVAL GUIDE

Kristen D. Hofheimer, Esq
Katherine Wilcox Carter, Esq.
and
B. Caitlin Walters, Esq

Printed in the United States of America

ISBN: 978-0-578-83006-3

Kristen D. Hofheimer,
A Tribute

The Women's Custody Survival Guide was first written and published by Kristen D. Hofheimer in 2009.

Though we've been aware for a while that our custody book was due for an update (and we've since updated almost all of our other titles!), it was a hard thing for us to bring ourselves to do. Kristen retired from the practice of law in 2017 after being diagnosed with Stage IV terminal breast cancer and passed away in January of 2019.

If you knew Kristen, consider yourself lucky. She truly was an exceptional human being and a fantastic family law attorney – one of the best in the state of Virginia, particularly when it came to handling complicated custody cases. She was kind, empathetic, and completely impossible to ruffle.

She was the former managing partner of Hofheimer Family Law Firm, and a visionary when it came to providing women with the information and inspiration needed to survive (and thrive!) through their family law cases. She founded our popular Girl's Night Out group as an opportunity for women going through a divorce or custody case to connect with other similarly situated women in a fun, social atmosphere (all completely paid for by the firm!). She created our Custody Bootcamp for Moms seminar program so that Virginia moms could learn all about what it takes to represent yourself at the juvenile court level in a custody and visitation case. She – literally – wrote the book (THIS book!) on Virginia custody and visitation cases in her easy-to-read, super informative *The Woman's Custody Survival Guide* which we're updating now – keeping her original content, and adding updates related to recent changes to the law.

As an attorney, she was top notch. There's no doubt that she was one of the best in Virginia, and that you'd be hard pressed to find a superior mind. Kristen was a former Barrister with the Hoffman-Panson American Inns of Court, former State Liaison for American Inns of Court, a member of the Virginia Trial

Lawyers Association, President of the Family Law Organization of Greater Hampton Roads, a member of the Virginia Beach Bar Association's Juvenile and Domestic Relations District Court's Bar/Bench Liaison Committee, and in 2008 & 2009 Super Lawyers named her as one of Virginia's Rising Stars. In short, her career was illustrious.

But she was so much more than that. It's difficult to find words to convey the totality of a person, but it's also impossible not to at least try. To me, personally, she was the woman who gave me my big break professionally, as a brand new attorney straight out of law school. She was always kind, encouraging, helpful, and more than willing to sit down and troubleshoot any issue I might be having.

She was the darling middle daughter of her parents, Charlie and Diane Hofheimer, the husband and wife attorney/paralegal team who founded the firm (along with partner Jack Ferrebee) and helped Kristen find her platform. During their time in practice, Charlie and Diane worked with Prevent Child Abuse Hampton Roads (now known as Champions for Children), and inspired Kristen to work with moms facing terrible custody cases. In fact, the three were featured in a documentary, *Small Justice: Little Justice in America's Courts*, for their work with protective moms.

She was the wife of Missy 'the Missile' Giove, a world champion downhill bike racer. In the last several years of her life, Kristen and Missy traveled extensively together, camping, hiking, and sightseeing (often with their Pomeranian, Dash, and their cat, Maybe). Kristen even requested that Missy compete in the 2015 Windham World Cup, the world downhill biking championship, after her diagnosis so that Kristen could see her win one more time. Without any training, and on a borrowed bike, Missy qualified. At the Championship, she placed 16th, all in an effort to help inspire Kristen. (She would have placed higher – in fact, she had the third fastest time at one point, but crashed in a qualifying race.) "We kinda went through some things that maybe she'd like to do in life, you know, and one was to see me race a World Cup," Missy said. "I was like, 'really?' I was like, 'OK!'"

Her son, Shay, recently married his childhood sweetheart, Morgan, and, in March of 2018, had Kristen's first grandson, Nova. Shay is Kristen's only child, and they shared an incredibly close bond. In fact, after Kristen's cancer diagnosis, the entire family – Charlie, Diane, Missy, Shay, and Morgan (who was pregnant at the time) moved down to Burnsville, North Carolina to "Hofheimer Holler" to be near Kristen's brother, R.D., and his two children, Mackenzie and Chase.

Kristen loved MixxedFit, a hip hop style dance fitness class, and found a second family in the tight knit group of women she encountered there. Even while undergoing extensive chemotherapy and radiation treatments, Kristen continued attending MixxedFit classes regularly.

Kristen also loved music (particularly Ani DiFranco), horses and horseback riding, the beach, karaoke, *Game of Thrones* (and specifically Daenerys Targaryen, the "mother of dragons"— though I sometimes wonder how she would feel about the series ending!), and dancing.

As an attorney, friend, daughter, sister, mother, and wife, Kristen will be missed, and we hope we can do her proud as we continue to use and update this title in part as a tribute to her memory, and in part as a recognition of how important this information is for Virginia women facing custody cases.

Kristen, we miss you, we love you, and we can't thank you enough for allowing us to be a part of your team. We'll always be grateful,

Katie & Caitlin

FORWARD

When I took the bar exam, Kristen sat just a few seats away from me. Hofheimer and Herrell – and I had no idea.

I didn't know, then, that Kristen was nearby, what a powerful force she was, what family she represented, or all the ways that the Hofheimers – Kristen, Charlie, and Diane – would change my life for the better.

Charlie Hofheimer originally hired me, even though he told me he didn't have any openings available for attorneys. I didn't mind; I was so hungry to prove myself, and so willing to do whatever it took that, well, here I am, more than 20 years later.

I had no idea, of course, as none of us ever really do, how my life would be shaped by these people, this firm, and the challenges of representing women exclusively in divorce and custody cases.

When Kristen was diagnosed with breast cancer for the second time in 2017, we were all heartbroken. But I knew that, no matter what, I was determined to keep the firm going – for the people who work here, who've become like my own family, and for the women who need our services.

Educating women about their rights in divorce and custody cases is vital work, and I was pleased, proud (and a little intimidated) to take over ownership of the firm in 2018. Even though the Hofheimers are gone – Charlie and Diane retired prior to Kristen's diagnosis – we still feel their influence keenly every day.

Working with women – battered women and protective mothers, stay at home wives, nursing moms, single mothers, working women, retirees, professionals, and so on – is our life's work. Providing education to help women make informed, productive, savvy decisions about their finances, their children, and their lives helps lift us all up.

I feel so fortunate to have known Charlie, Kristen, and Diane (Charlie's wife, and both Charlie and Kristen's former paralegal). It has shaped me, as a woman, as a mother, as an attorney, and as an advocate for women. It has given meaning to my life and influences me every single day as I make decisions about the future of the firm and the scope of the projects we undertake.

Revising this book is one of the ways I hope to bring the firm into the future. In this version, we've included updated sections on changes in Virginia laws as it relates to custody, working with Guardians ad litem (who, when it comes to custody cases, are definitely VIPs!), support guidelines, military families, and more.

Custody and visitation are kind of complicated – not so much in the general, overall concepts (like 'best interests of the child'), but in how rules are applied, how standards are changing and evolving, and what judges, guardians ad litem, and attorneys understand about the process that may be foreign to you.

Together with two other attorneys, Caitlin Walters and Katie Wilcox Carter, we've put a lot of work into this newest edition of Kristen's original custody book. We want to help make sure that you feel in control of your own future, so that you can make the best possible decisions for yourself and your family, even in the most difficult circumstances. We kept a lot of Kristen's original work, too, because we weren't sure that it could really be improved upon – but we updated to include content that is more specifically targeted to some of the recent issues we've seen in the Virginia juvenile and circuit courts.

We're here, too, should you need help litigating or negotiating your upcoming custody case. If your case is part of an underlying divorce, I recommend attending our Second Saturday seminar (now offered on Zoom!). If yours is a pure custody case – whether custody, visitation, and/or child support petitions have been filed, or if you're modifying an already-existing custody agreement or court order – then our Custody Bootcamp for Moms is a great place for you to get additional information.

Whether you ultimately choose to become a client of the firm or not, we're here to help make sure you have as thorough an understanding as possible. It's what Kristen would have wanted and it's definitely part of all of our life's work here at Hofheimer Family Law.

I hope you find what you're looking for within the pages of this book. If you need any more information, want to enroll in a seminar, need to be pointed in the right direction, or hope to schedule a consultation, I hope you'll reach out to us. You're in the right place, and we're here to help.

Thank you for being a part of our mission, and for taking the steps to educate and empower yourself or someone you love.

Sheera R. Herrell

Child Custody Survival Guide

TABLE OF CONTENTS

WARNING AND DISCLAIMER

This book is based on Virginia law. While various jurisdictions in Virginia and outside of it may have similar laws and processes related to child custody, the reader will find this book most helpful for general informational purposes. This book is not intended to be used as specific legal advice. Please consult with an attorney licensed in your local jurisdiction with significant experience in family law for specific legal advice regarding your child custody case.

INTRODUCTION

If you are in a custody dispute or think you may be headed there, you will find this book invaluable. Chapters 1 through 3 explain the basics: what custody really means and how it is determined, as well as when and how custody and visitation can be changed. In discussing the various custody factors, this book will give you tips about what specific kinds of information the court will be looking for, what facts can help or hurt your case, and how to present evidence in your case in support of each custody factor. Chapter 4 addresses several special issues that arise in child custody cases. If one of these special issues applies to your case, Chapter 4 will give you suggestions about how to best address your special issue and what evidence and witnesses may be key to winning your case. Chapter 5 discusses alternatives to litigation and why resolving your case outside of the courtroom, with the help of a mediator or collaborative team, may produce a better result for your family than anything a judge could rule.

Chapter 6 of this book is your courtroom survival guide. This chapter will tell you what every woman wishes her attorney would take the time to tell her in detail about court, including tips that can make or break your case. You will learn what to wear, what to expect, when to stand, and when to speak. You will learn the format of a custody trial and why you are always rushing to the courthouse and then having to wait. In addition, you will learn what to do and what not to do in order to survive cross-examination.

In Chapter 7, you will learn valuable (and money-saving) suggestions for working with your attorney. You will also learn important considerations for working with a guardian *ad litem* and other professionals involved in your case. For women who choose to represent themselves (or are forced to do so because of finances), Chapter 8 will give you the basics for acting as your own attorney. You will learn how to come to court prepared to present your evidence like an attorney and how to tell your story in an organized and persuasive manner. Chapter 9 will distill the information in this book to the short list – the 10 most important things to remember in your custody and visitation case. After reading this book, you will be empowered with insight and information about child custody so that you can walk confidently into the courtroom and present your case persuasively.

If you read this book and still need more information, visit our website *www.hoflaw.com* for up-to-date divorce and custody blogs, articles, and videos. You may also attend one of our upcoming live custody workshops. Please see our website for details.

CHAPTER 1: WHAT IS CHILD CUSTODY?

What does "child custody" mean?

In Virginia, there are two types of custody: **legal custody** and **physical custody**. When we talk about **child custody** in general, we're touching on both of these kinds of custody.

Legal custody has to do with having the authority to make major decisions affecting the child in question.

Physical custody has to do with where and with whom the child resides. **Visitation,** or **parenting time,** determines how and when a parent without physical custody of a child sees the child.

Legal Custody

Legal custody can be awarded solely to one parent or jointly to both.

Sole custody means one parent can make the major decisions impacting the child's life without input from the other parent. For this reason, because legal custody is considered to be absolutely central to raising a child and being a parent, legal custody is almost always awarded jointly.

When parents have joint legal custody, they are expected to discuss major decisions and try to reach consensus. Virginia courts consider decisions regarding education, non-emergency medical care, and religious upbringing to be major decisions on which joint custodians should reach agreement.

18

What happens when parents disagree, but they have joint legal custody?

As you can probably imagine, it happens! Disputes arise frequently, but those three things (non-emergency medical care, religious upbringing, and education) are the only areas where cooperation on decision-making is required.

So, what comes up? Predictable things. For the most part, parents fight over whether their children are going to go to public or private school. Although fights in other areas are less frequent, we do sometimes see fights about medical care (especially in the context of vaccinations), or occasionally religious upbringing. Generally, though, these areas are ones where, once the die is cast, there's not a whole lot of going back on it. If your kids have always been vaccinated, or have always attended, say, a Methodist church, chances are pretty good that you're not going to have a whole lot of issues come up. It's possible, I guess – but not all that likely.

But what if against all odds it *does* come up, and you just can't agree? No amount of talking it out is going to resolve these fundamental differences, you just don't have an agreement. It's hard to have a consensus when it's essentially one versus one; there's no one to cast the tie-breaking vote.

There's nothing left but to take your case to the judge and let him decide. Hopefully it won't come to that, but, if it does, it's really the only thing you can do to move the case forward. Obviously, in the case of school registration, time is of the essence, which probably doesn't make things any easier.

Physical Custody

Physical custody has to do with where and with whom a child resides. Physical custody can be **primary physical custody** (sometimes called **sole physical custody**), **shared physical custody** (sometimes called **joint physical custody**), or **split physical custody**. Additionally, some people prefer to use the term "**parenting plan**" rather than "custody" to describe the physical custodial arrangement.

19

Primary physical custody means that the child lives primarily with one parent and has visitation with the other parent. Shared physical custody means an arrangement by which both parents spend significant amounts of time with the child. The parents may have equal time with the child, but not necessarily. Shared custody may refer to many different sorts of arrangements under which each parent has the child for a good portion of the time.

Under the child support guidelines, **shared custody** refers to a situation in which the parent without primary physical custody spends over ninety days per year with the child. In determining how many days the visiting parent has, the Virginia code has specific definitions for what counts. A day is defined as a 24-hour period of time; so, a weekend from 6:00pm on Friday until 6:00pm on Sunday would count as two days. If the parent has an overnight visit of less than 24 hours, it counts as half a day. For example, if the parent picks up the child from school on a Wednesday, keeps him overnight, and returns him on Thursday morning, that period of time counts as half a day for shared custody child support purposes. Any visit that does not include overnight visitation does not count at all for purposes of determining the number of days per year of visitation. It is important to note that the ninety-day requirement and the definition of a day are only important in determining child support. There is no ninety-day requirement for determining whether a custody arrangement is or is not called shared custody for purposes of determining custody and visitation.

Split custody refers to a scenario in which parents have more than one child together, and the custodial arrangement is not the same for each child. For instance, if the parents had two children and the mother had primary physical custody of one of the children and the father had primary physical custody of the other child, it would be considered split custody. Courts typically do not like to split up siblings. Often when parents have a split custody arrangement, it is because the parents determined for themselves that split custody was best for their family rather than because a judge ordered it. However, there are situations when a court will order split custody. We might see this outcome, then, when an older and mature teenage child has a strong preference to live with a parent other than the one that the court determines is best for the younger children.

What does the court prefer in terms of custodial arrangements?

In July of 2018, the law regarding custody was revised. The statute now specifically provides that "[t]here shall be no presumption in favor of any form of custody."

Based on wording alone, I'm not sure that this represents any real legal change at all. I was actually already under the impression that judges considered all the different kinds of custodial arrangements more or less equally and applied whatever they believed to be appropriate to the case at hand.

In fact, I think the wording here is clear. No one type of custody – primary, shared, or split – will be elevated above the others in terms of importance. The judge will consider any and all possible custodial arrangements equally. I guess, if I'm being pedantic, it doesn't say that they necessarily have to be considered equally, just that one kind of custody won't be favored above the others.

But what does that actually mean in practice?

Father's rights groups say that this means that dads will have equal opportunity in court. The longstanding assumption (I'm not saying that I believe this to be a correct assumption) was that mothers received preferential treatment in courts where custody was concerned.

I think that model – the model favoring moms – has actually been in the process of being reversed for a number of years though. I wouldn't say at all that moms receive preferential treatment in custody cases. In fact, I find that moms fare worse in court, or, at least, they bear far more scrutiny. A mom with a boyfriend, for example, is looked at far more negatively than a dad with a girlfriend.

I do believe it's probably reasonable to suggest that this means we will see a rise in cases where shared custody is ordered. (Shared custody, just to refresh your memory, is any custodial arrangement where the non-custodial parent – the parent who has the child less – has 90 or more days in a calendar year with the child.)

But wait – the statute says that no one particular kind of custodial arrangement is preferred over the others!

Yeah, I know! But I think there is a difference between what the statute says, and how the judges are interpreting it. At a (relatively) recent continuing education seminar I attended, a panel of three judges (each from different courts and representing both juvenile and circuit courts) all indicated that they believed that the new law required them to consider shared custody first. I know, I know – that's not actually what it says at all. It says no one kind of custody should be presumed, and that should include shared custody.

I think, though, that it doesn't. Shared custody is where most analysis starts these days. Maybe there isn't a legal precedent for this based on the exact wording of the statute, but I think it's probably fair to say that this is most likely what it means – or what the judges are taking it to mean.

After all, child custody decisions are based on judicial analysis of the best interests of the child factors, which can lead to wide ranging decisions that are based quite heavily on the prejudices (both good and bad) of the individual judges involved.

As you can probably already tell, it's pretty loosey goosey – and very much down to judicial interpretation.

But aren't there cases where shared custody wouldn't be appropriate?

Oh my goodness, of course! While the answer is certainly yes, it's all going to be down to the evidence you provide, and how well you convince the judge based on those best interests of the child factors, that something other than shared custody would be more appropriate in your case.

It's definitely worth working with a lawyer; there are a lot of presumptions to overcome here. As sad as it is to say, it's becoming more and more difficult all the time, so coming up with a specific strategy and working with an attorney who is experienced in handling divorce and custody cases is going to be even more critical than ever before.

Visitation

Visitation (sometimes referred to as **parenting time**) refers to the time that the parent without physical custody spends with the child. Typically, visitation includes overnight and extended periods of time spent with the non-custodial parent in his or her home or the place of his or her choosing; however, in special circumstances, visitation can be supervised or can take place in a therapeutic setting.

What is a typical visitation schedule?

Well, first off, let me say: there is no such thing as a "typical" visitation schedule. Although there are some arrangements that courts (and parents) favor over others, there are literally as many different types of arrangements with respect to visitation as there are parents and children out there in the world. There's no right or wrong way, really – though that's not to suggest that if a court orders a specific custody arrangement, you'll necessarily love the way your parenting time is divided with your child's father.

Remember that physical custody can be split three ways: primary to one parent, shared between both parents, or split.

Primary Physical Custody

In a primary physical custody scenario, the non-custodial parent (the parent who has the children less) has 89 or fewer days in a calendar year.

If there ever was a "typical" custody schedule, I think it was this one: every other weekend, Wednesday night dinner, two weeks in the summer, and alternating holidays. That would be less than 90 days in a year, and it would fall under the primary physical custody heading. This is still a popular custodial arrangement today, but it is by no means the only custodial arrangement, or even the custodial arrangement most preferred by judges.

If you and your child's father don't live near each other, sharing the children every other weekend isn't necessarily the easiest thing in the world to do. It could also be a primary physical custody arrangement if you guys are geographically separated, and the non-custodial parent gets the kids for a larger chunk of time in the summer. Even if it's a VERY large chunk of time in the summer, it might still be hard to get to that 90-day threshold.

Remember, now, that judges must consider all forms of custody equally, so they're looking at shared custody with at least equal preference.

Shared Physical Custody

In a shared physical custody arrangement, the non-custodial parent has 90 or more days in a calendar year, so there are even more different variations of how custody could be shared between two parents under this model.

We see a lot of week on/week off custody, and it's probably safe to say that this is an arrangement that judges tend to like. At any rate, it's easy to understand, though you may be feeling that this may or may not be the best arrangement for children who are in school.

We see parents share days on an alternating schedule, too – say, 4-3-3-4, or something similar. We also sometimes have parents where one parent has the children during the week, and another has the children on the weekend.

A lot has to do with each parent's work schedule, and the time that they have to devote to the children during a given time. For, say, a military parent who is deployable, or a parent who travels a considerable portion of the time, it may be that a typical arrangement like week on/week off, or 4-3-3-4 doesn't work so well.

What if my child's father doesn't want a consistent schedule?

If your child's father's schedule is weird, you may find that your custodial schedule is similarly unusual. It may not seem fair that you have to continually rearrange your life because his is inconsistent (that's a frequent complaint I get from military wives, especially), but his ability to be present in the children's lives is an argument that the court often finds pretty compelling. You'll likely have to offer make up time to accommodate for, say, his drill schedule or various deployments, which harkens back to those best interests of the child factors, which we will discuss in greater detail in the next chapter.

Though you may have to be flexible more often than you'd like (especially given his rigidity when, say, you ask to trade dates or for more time), I often find that it's more advantageous, when it comes to custody, to be the parent with the more consistent schedule. It often does mean that, by default, you get more time simply because you are more available.

Rights of First Refusal

We can also include, whether in custody arrangements ordered in court or in agreements that we reach, rights of first refusal. A right of first refusal is when you say that the other parent must be offered the child before the child is placed in the care of a babysitter or other non-parent (like a grandparent) if a biological parent is unable to care for the child for a period of a certain number of hours (4 or 8 or even 24). If your child's father's plan is to get as much time as possible (to keep his child support obligation low) and then delegate that time, say, to his mother (who you never liked in the first place), a right of first refusal might be a good inclusion for you.

Courts like rights of first refusal because they maximize the amount of time that a parent is able to care for the child, instead of having the child in daycare or in the care of a non-parent.

Split Physical Custody

Split physical custody is unusual, mostly because judges don't like to split up siblings. It can happen, though, and not just in movies! (Hey, we all saw "The Parent Trap", right?)

Though it's rare that it would be a *true* "Parent Trap" arrangement where one parent had one child and the other parent kept the other child, and they *never* saw each other or the other child (yikes – sounds terrible, doesn't it?), that is one possibility. More likely, though, the parents trade the children around at intervals, with them spending some time with both parents, and some time overlapping with the siblings as well.

I've seen a judge do it in at least one case, but most often when this happens, it's because the parents agree to it. I see it mostly where one sibling has special needs that make what is appropriate for him different from what is appropriate for the other siblings.

If this sounds ideal to you, it's probably a good idea to enlist the support of a lawyer to get some tips about how to get a split physical custody arrangement in place.

What does "parenting time" mean?

We often use the term "parenting time" to describe the time that either parent has with the children. Where "visitation" came to have a sort of ugly connotation (in the sense that the non-custodial parent was just *visiting*, as opposed to actually *parenting*), "parenting time" was adopted as a nicer, more politically correct way of describing the division of time between two parents.

So much of what an attorney does is semantic. Words matter. If you're talking about the children, it's a good idea to say "our" children and describe dad's time as "parenting time." Talking about how you want to effectively co-parent can go a long way as well. Show the court – and your child's father – that you intend to keep him present in your child's life, and carefully select your words to reflect that intent. It's important to a judge to know that you will be able to co-parent, so you need to show your maturity here. Words matter!

Can I ask that he have supervised visitation?

It's possible but probably unlikely. Without a history of abuse or neglect, a diagnosed mental health or addiction problem, or something similar, it'll probably be hard to convince the court that supervised visitation is necessary.

Also, *who* supervises? In some cases, the judge is satisfied with dad's mother being the supervisor (which often presents its own problems). In the event that visitation occurs in a facility, or with a specific supervisor, these interactions can be challenging to schedule – not to mention expensive!

If you're wondering whether he'd get supervised visitation just because he's never cared for the child alone before, or because he is a careless and immature, you'll likely be disappointed.

If supervised visitation is important to you, you'll want to talk to an attorney sooner rather than later. Be prepared to discuss your concerns and bring with you any proof you might have of any issues that might translate into him being unable to be alone with your children.

CHAPTER 2: How Do Courts Decide Child Custody and Visitation?

In Virginia, as in most states, child custody and visitation determinations are made based upon the idea of the "best interests of the child." The court looks at specific factors with respect to the parents and the child in question. After analyzing the factors, the court's task is to make a custody and visitation determination which serves the best interests of the child. In Virginia, these factors are as follows:

Child custody and visitation factors
1. The age and physical and mental condition of the child, giving due consideration to the child's changing developmental needs;
2. The age and physical and mental condition of each parent;
3. The relationship existing between each parent and each child, giving due consideration to the positive involvement with the child's life, the ability to accurately assess and meet the emotional, intellectual and physical needs of the child;
4. The needs of the child, giving due consideration to other important relationships of the child, including but not limited to siblings, peers and extended family members;

5. The role that each parent has played and will play in the future, in the upbringing and care of the child;

6. The propensity of each parent to actively support the child's contact and relationship with the other parent, including whether a parent has unreasonably denied access to or visitation with the child;

7. The relative willingness and demonstrated ability of each parent to maintain a close and continuing relationship with the child, and the ability of each parent to cooperate in and resolve disputes regarding matters affecting the child;

8. The reasonable preference of the child, if the court deems the child to be of reasonable intelligence, understanding, age and experience to express such a preference;

9. Any history of family abuse. Family abuse is defined as any act involving violence, force, or threat including, but not limited to, any forceful detention, which results in bodily injury or places one in reasonable apprehension of bodily injury and which is committed by a person against such person's family or household member. If the court finds such a history, the court may disregard [factor #6].

10. Such other factors as the court deems necessary and proper to the determination.

In this chapter, I will discuss each of these factors in detail, including what evidence the court will be interested in when analyzing each factor.

Factor #1: The age and physical and mental condition of the child, giving due consideration to the child's changing developmental needs.

In analyzing this factor, the court is interested in the child herself. How old is she? Does she have any health issues that the court should be considering? What about any emotional or intellectual special needs? What are the child's specific developmental needs at this time, and what developmental needs will be arising in the foreseeable future? You will need to be prepared to address these questions in an organized manner by presenting **admissible evidence**. As much as you would like to put all of your information in front of the judge, courts are only permitted to view, hear, and consider evidence which is considered admissible under the rules of evidence. I will briefly discuss basics of evidence in this book, including the rule that you will probably have to deal with the most: the **hearsay** rule. Please refer to the **What is Hearsay?** section of this book for more on the hearsay rule.

If your child is healthy and has no special needs, this factor will be easy to address. You may just need to brush up on some of your child-rearing reference books in order to articulate what you believe to be your child's current and foreseeable developmental needs (such as attachment, intellectual stimulation, socialization with peers). If you have a child with special needs, you will need to be able to present your child's special needs to the court, and you will likely need to use an expert witness to testify about your child's special needs and how those needs are best met. If your child is an infant or a toddler, breastfeeding and attachment are issues that may need to be addressed here. I will discuss the issue of **custody and visitation with a breastfeeding child** in the **Special Issues in Child Custody** section of this book. Attachment and separation anxiety are issues that may need to be addressed by an attachment expert. If your child is school age, you may wish to present evidence regarding which custody and visitation arrangement will best promote your child's academic and social success in school. With a teenager, you may choose to present evidence about your child's wishes (see more under factor #8), or about how a proposed custody arrangement will impact his significant extracurricular activities. Factor #1 is all about your child, who she is, and what she needs.

Factor #2: The age and physical and mental condition of each parent.

The court must consider the age and physical and mental condition of each parent. Generally, the age and physical condition of the parents are not major issues. So long as each parent is capable of providing care for the child, the court is not going to award custody to the parent who is younger or more physically fit. The mental condition of the parents is another story.

The Virginia courts and legislature have gone around and around in the last several years on the issue of whether a parent's therapy records, and/or testimony by a therapist regarding a parent, can be obtained or is admissible as evidence in a child custody case. As of July 1, 2008, the statute which kept these records confidential and inadmissible in custody cases was repealed, and the records and/or testimony may be admissible due to the fact that the mental condition of the parents is a factor that the courts are required to consider.

Often, if the mental health of a parent is at issue, the court will order a psychological evaluation of one or both parents. Additionally, expert witnesses can provide testimony about mental health issues. Be forewarned that although you can give testimony about behaviors that you have witnessed on the part of your child's father, *you* cannot diagnose him as being mentally ill. Only a qualified mental health evaluator or provider can do that. Attempts on your own to portray or describe your child's father as "crazy" may end up backfiring against you and make you look vindictive. If you are concerned about the mental health of your child's father, you may want to consider requesting a psychological evaluation of him, but only after careful consultation with your attorney. If you request a psychological evaluation of him, he will probably request one of you. Psychological testing is not foolproof. Your spouse may come out with flying colors, even if he is not psychologically sound. On the other hand, you may come out as having some traits of concern simply by virtue of the stress and fear that the custody litigation is causing you. A biased evaluator or skewed test data can cause irreparable damage to your custody case.

Factor #3: The relationship existing between each parent and each child, giving due consideration to the positive involvement with the child's life, the ability to accurately assess and meet the emotional, intellectual, and physical needs of the child.

This factor addresses the quality of the relationship between each child and each parent. While courts are usually reluctant to make a custody determination which separates siblings from one another, it is not uncommon for children in a family to differ in the quality of their relationships with each respective parent. The quality of one child's relationship with a parent may impact a custody determination for all of the children in a family, if the relationship is profoundly positive or negative. If there is an unusually strong bond between a parent and one or more children, it is important that the court sees that the relationship is an appropriate parent/child relationship, not a peer-type friendship and not one in which the child is providing comfort and support to the parent. You must be extremely careful – especially if your relationship with the other parent ended due to his infidelity or you are simply devastated by the breakup – that you are not putting your child in the role of confidant and emotional nurturer. Additionally, mothers are particularly susceptible to being accused of being "enmeshed" with their children. Therefore, while you want to portray for the court the positive and unique qualities of your relationships with each of your children, you must take care to demonstrate that you observe appropriate parent/child boundaries in those relationships.

When courts do allow children to testify or to speak to the judge in chambers, the court is more likely to ask them about their relationship with each parent, rather than asking them directly which parent should have custody. In these situations, the court is usually more interested in hearing from the child about her relationship with each parent and how each parent is able to assess and meet the child's various needs, than which parent the child wants to live with. The court is tasked with making a decision based upon what the court determines to be in the best interest of the child, not necessarily on what the child wants. This is a factor for which a child may be able to give the court significant insight.

In order to demonstrate to the court that you are able to accurately assess and meet the child's emotional, intellectual and physical needs, you should be able to articulate to the court what you think those needs are, and how, as custodian of the child, you plan to meet those needs. You may also wish to call witnesses, such as teachers, counselors, and health care providers to testify about their assessment of what the child's needs are and their observations of your ability to accurately assess and meet those needs. If you have a special needs child, this factor may be of particular significance in your case. The court will be interested in how well-equipped you are to deal with your child's specific needs and challenges.

Factor #4: The needs of the child, giving due consideration to other important relationships of the child, including but not limited to siblings, peers, and extended family members.

This factor focuses on the child's needs, particularly with respect to continuing the child's important relationships. You will want to provide evidence that shows that, in your custody, the child will be able to maintain his relationships with neighborhood and school friends, siblings (including step and half siblings), grandparents, aunts, uncles, cousins, and anyone else who has played an important role in your child's life. You may want to have a neighbor testify about her child's relationship with your child or perhaps make a map of the neighborhood showing the proximity of all of the children that your child plays with. You may wish to have your parents or siblings testify about your extended family activities and traditions and their unique relationships with your child.

Factor #5: The role that each parent has played and will play in the future, in the upbringing and care of the child.

This is the factor under which the parent who has been the primary caretaker of the children should get some credit. Often, women mistakenly think that the court will award them custody without much of a challenge because they have been the ones to

33

care for their children, from prenatal care to hourly infant feedings, to diaper changing, to pediatrician visits, to being there when the school bus comes, to providing a snack and homework help or being the one to miss work when a child is home with the flu; while the children's father had minimal involvement in the day-to-day aspects of child-rearing. Wrong!!! This is but one of the ten factors that courts consider when awarding child custody; however, this is the factor in which, for most families, women prevail. Make the most of it! You will likely have a whole lot of information about your role as the children's primary caretaker. You could probably go on for hours – if not days – about the things that you have done for your child from the day she was born, things which no one else in the universe, including your child's father, had any interest in doing. Yet, you can also count on the fact that the court is not going to give you days, or probably even hours, to give this testimony. Because of this, it is very important to organize your information in such a way that you can present it in court in an abbreviated manner without discounting its importance.

If you are working with an attorney, you should write a narrative for your attorney outlining all of the things that you have done and continue to do for your child. You should also make sure to let your attorney know the things that your child's father has done and continues to do, so that your attorney will not be caught by surprise in court. If you have a guardian *ad litem* or custody evaluator, you may also wish to provide this narrative to them. However, if you are providing documentation to a guardian *ad litem* or custody evaluator, you should self-edit more than you need to with your own attorney; be straight-forward, factual, and brief rather than providing a rambling narrative. Focus on your strengths, rather than your child's father's weaknesses, and, above all, do not provide the guardian *ad litem* or custody evaluator with a lengthy, written diatribe about the faults and shortcomings of your child's father. To do so will probably make you, rather than the other parent, look bad in the eyes of these people who have a significant voice in your case.

Whether or not you are working with an attorney, you should be able to summarize in your testimony who takes care of the basics in child rearing:

1. Who gets the children up, fed, and off to school/daycare in the morning?
2. Who makes the doctor/dentist/therapy appointments and takes the children to the appointments?
3. Who stays home when a child is sick?
4. Who finds and registers for summer camps, sports, and lessons?
5. Who helps with homework?
6. Who feeds the children dinner?
7. Who bathes them?
8. Who puts them to bed?
9. Who goes to parent/teacher conferences?
10. Who makes sure the children have clean clothes that fit when they have to be dressed for an occasion?
11. Who plans birthday parties and holiday activities for the children?
12. Who arranges play dates?

This is a factor for which you will probably be your most important witness. You may choose to call lay witnesses, such as teachers, neighbors, and friends to corroborate your testimony about your involvement with your children. Other corroborating evidence can include school records (who signed the report cards and homework log?), calendars, medical records (who brought in the children?), and daycare records (who signed the children in and out?), although you will need to work within the rules of evidence to get these records admitted into evidence in court. Another method of organizing this information in a way that makes it easy for the court to comprehend is to make a chart of the child care activities and what percentage of responsibility each parent has for each activity. If you and your child's father have been living separately for some period of time, it may also be helpful to make a pie-chart of the time the child has spent living with the two of you together and living with each parent separately.

Factor #6: The propensity of each parent to actively support the child's contact and relationship with the other parent, including whether a parent has unreasonably denied access to or visitation with the child.

This is one of Virginia's two "friendly parent" factors. Many jurisdictions require courts to consider which parent is more likely to cooperate with the other parent and promote the relationship between the child and the other parent. Many judges will say that they consider the friendly parent factors to be the most important in making custody/visitation decisions. Mothers often get tripped up on the friendly parent provisions. This is frequently due to the fact that during the marriage or relationship with the child's father, most or all of the child-rearing responsibilities were delegated to the mother. She handled healthcare, dental care, and therapy issues for the children on her own. She went to school functions, PTA meetings, and parent-teacher conferences on her own. She scheduled play dates and recreational activities on her own. During the marriage or relationship, it never occurred to anyone that the fact that she did these things on her own meant that she was trying to deprive the father of his relationship with his child. She was simply fulfilling her responsibilities within the family unit. Chances are, if this was the family division of labor, the father never asked about doctor and dentist appointments or PTA meetings. These were chores. Post-separation, it makes sense that the mother would not change the way in which she took care of child-rearing tasks. However, this same approach to child-rearing responsibilities, post-separation, could result in an accusation that the mother is trying to alienate the child from the father and make her appear to be an "unfriendly parent."

Additionally, in highly contested cases, the father will set a "friendly parent trap." Remember, the court must consider whether a parent has unreasonably denied access to or visitation with the child. In order to make you look as if you do not support his contact with the child or have unreasonably denied him access, he will start making requests for contact like never before. If you have custody, he may suddenly begin asking for an extra night each week, or to bring the child home at an unreasonable hour on a school night. If he currently has custody, he will create a situation which makes it extremely inconvenient for you to exercise your visit. If you acquiesce, the requests will keep coming, like the mouse who first only wanted a cookie and then needed a glass of milk, etc., until you finally have to say no. If, on the other hand, you react negatively, he will use that reaction as proof that you do not support his contact with the child.

If your child's father begins putting you on the spot with requests, you should take some time to think out and/or discuss with your attorney how you should respond. It is fine to say to him that you need some time to look at your calendar and think about whether the idea is best for your child. Discuss the request with your attorney and decide whether it is best to give in and show how unremittingly reasonable you are, or whether you should take a deep breath and counter with a calm, "No, I do not think it would be best for Junior to attend the Wet Tee-Shirt Competition with you this Wednesday night, but he would probably enjoy going to the Children's Museum with you right after school on Wednesday." It is always a good idea, when turning down an unreasonable request, to give a reasonable counter-offer. If you can do it in writing (e-mail is always easy), then you will have a record of your efforts to allow him reasonable time with the child if he ever accuses you of failing to support his contact with the child.

Even if your child's father had no interest in your child's school, health care, and extracurricular activities while you were together, once you enter the world of child custody litigation, you can expect that he will suddenly become fiercely interested. It is to your benefit, no matter how cumbersome it sounds, to share information about these things with him, and to do so in a timely manner. If you take the time to do this, and he still remains uninvolved, so be it. That fact will help you in your custody case. If he suddenly starts showing up at every teeth cleaning appointment and camp physical wearing his "World's Greatest Dad" tee-shirt, try not to lose your composure. He now has an attorney instructing him how to be a parent (funny how he listens to his attorney's advice on how to raise your child more than he ever listened to yours...). Resist the temptation to say something sarcastic. If you do, you will undoubtedly hear the same words repeated in court. And the judge's sense of humor is probably not as keen as yours. Try to take yourself out of the equation and focus on how glad your child must be to suddenly have dad observing his every flouride treatment and height and weight measurement.

If you are under a court order to provide specific visitation, consult with an attorney before you ever withhold a court-ordered visit, even if you believe that you have very good reason to do so (see chapter 4 on abuse), as to do so can have dire consequences for your custody case. If there is an issue that you think justifies withholding visitation, try to set an emergency hearing on the issue before the next scheduled visit.

Because the friendly parent provisions tend to work against the parent who has had the most responsibility for the child, it is very important that women be wary of friendly parent traps and make efforts, within reason, to support and promote the father/child relationship. It is also important to be able to counter claims that you have not promoted the relationship by documenting your efforts via e-mail or by keeping them contemporaneously on a calendar.

Factor #7: The relative willingness and demonstrated ability of each parent to maintain a close and continuing relationship with the child, and the ability of each parent to cooperate in and resolve disputes regarding matters affecting the child.

This is the other friendly parent factor. It is sort of a disjointed one because the first part is concerned with whether each parent has maintained a relationship with the child, which does not seem to have a lot to do with each parent's ability to cooperate in and resolve disputes regarding the child. For the first part, which is somewhat diluted by the second, you simply need to present evidence that you have continued to keep a close relationship with the child and are willing to continue to do so. If the father has been an absentee parent, whether you and he were together or not, you would want to present that evidence, as well.

Again, judges seem to place particular emphasis on the friendly parent provisions. Generally, judges have little tolerance for parents who are unable to reach compromises between themselves in the rearing of their child. While this makes sense, there are situations in which it is unrealistic and unfair to expect a parent to be able to resolve disputes with the other parent without outside intervention. In cases of domestic violence, or where a parent is controlling or narcissistic, there is no level playing field in which real cooperation and dispute resolution can take place. What does take place is bullying and succumbing to a bully, which serves only the bully's interests and not the child's.

If there is a level playing field then, by all means cooperate and resolve disputes wherever possible. Keep a journal, log, or calendar in which you can document your efforts to cooperate. Keep e-mail communications which shows your efforts to compromise and resolve disputes. These can be important pieces of evidence for this factor. If there is not a level playing field, and you are not able to work together to resolve disputes, you will need to be able to justify this. Please see my comments under Factor #9 if there is a history of domestic violence. If you are dealing with narcissistic or controlling behavior, you will need to put on evidence to show the judge this behavior and why it inhibits you from being able to resolve disputes.

Often, if you are trying to parent with a controller or narcissist, you will be able to find e-mails or other communications in which your child's father shows his true colors. These e-mails, in his own words, are worth a thousand of your words in trying to explain his behavior to the court. Keep any abusive, controlling, or berating e-mails that he sends to you. They are invaluable for use in cross-examining an abusive, controlling, or narcissistic parent who claims that you do not cooperate with him in resolving disputes.

Factor #8: The reasonable preference of the child, if the court deems the child to be of reasonable

intelligence, understanding, age, and experience to express such a preference.

I am often asked how old a child must be in order to be able to choose which parent he wants to live with. The simple answer is 18. As long as a child is a minor, it is up to the court (if the parents cannot agree), not the child, to determine the child's best interest and make a custody decision accordingly. With that being said, though, judges vary on the issue of whether and under what circumstances they will allow children to give their input, and how much weight to give that input.

If the child has a guardian *ad litem*, who is an attorney appointed to represent the best interests of the child (please see the section on guardians *ad litem* in Chapter 7), your judge may not want to hear from the child. The judge may only want to hear what the guardian *ad litem* has to say. The guardian *ad litem* is supposed to let the court know the child's wishes even if those wishes are contrary to what the guardian *ad litem* recommends.

The court is supposed to allow your child to testify in open court if you choose to call her as a witness. If both parents agree, the judge may speak to the child in chambers without the parents or their attorneys present. In that case, the guardian *ad litem* will probably be present, as well as a court reporter to take down what is said in chambers. While this is the protocol which is supposed to be followed, some judges do it differently. The court is supposed to make a determination that the child is of reasonable intelligence, understanding, age and experience to give the court input. Often, courts decide that around the age of 12, it is appropriate to speak to children. Typically, the older a child is, the more weight the court will give to her preference. Most courts will acknowledge that once a child is old enough to drive, it does not make much sense to order her to live in a home where she clearly does not want to be, absent extraordinary circumstances.

Factor #9: Any history of family abuse. Family abuse is defined as any act involving violence, force, or threat including but not limited to any forceful

detention which results in bodily injury or places one in reasonable apprehension of bodily injury and which is committed by a person against such person's family or household member. If the court finds such a history, the court may disregard Factor #6.

The court is supposed to consider whether there is a history of family abuse in making child custody and visitation determinations. If you are able to prove to the court's satisfaction that there is a history of abuse, then the court may disregard the factor which requires you to promote the relationship between the child and the other parent, with the idea being that it is not reasonable to require a parent to support an abusive relationship. (I discuss the issue of custody and visitation determinations in cases where there has been abuse in the chapter in this book devoted to special issues in child custody). You should be aware that when you raise the issue of family abuse, the abuser is likely to not only deny that he is abusive, but also to claim that you are making a "false allegation" of abuse with the intent of depriving him of a relationship with his child. As I will further explain in the section on abuse, it is extremely important to proceed with caution when raising the issue of abuse. If possible, you should work with an attorney who has significant experience in dealing with issues of abuse in child custody cases, and you should also make sure that you have sufficient admissible evidence of the abuse so that you can counter any claim that you are making a false abuse allegation.

Factor #10: Such other factors as the court deems necessary and proper to the determination.

This factor is the catch-all for other issues which may be important to the court in determining child custody. Under this factor, the court may consider any special facts or circumstances in your case that the court deems relevant to making a custody and visitation determination regarding your child. Such circumstances will be discussed in-depth in the Special Issues in Child Custody section of this book.

Once the court has heard evidence and argument, it will make a child custody and visitation determination based upon the ten custody factors. The court must consider the factors but does not need to specifically state what weight was given to each factor. Because of the number and breadth of the factors, the court has a great deal of discretion in making child custody determinations.

Circuit Court versus Juvenile Court: Which is better for me?

Custody cases can take different shapes depending on what the underlying issues are. Basically, there are two types – custody where you and the child's father weren't married, and custody where you're also getting a divorce.

Why does it matter if we are also getting a divorce? Isn't a custody case the same regardless?

The basic issues in a custody case are the same regardless. You'll have to either agree to or let the judge decide how custody (legal and physical, we'll get to that in a minute) and visitation will be handled. But that's where the similarities end.

A divorce gives you a few more options – or, at least, to start with it seems that way. You can either file for custody, visitation, and child support in the juvenile court, or you can go ahead and file for divorce in the circuit court and get it all taken care of at once.

Is juvenile court or circuit court better for me?

This is a tricky question. It's not really that one court or another is better or worse; however, there are advantages and disadvantages depending on which court you find yourself in.

Juvenile and Domestic Relations District Court

Juvenile court is both less formal and more user friendly. If you're attempting to resolve custody issues without an attorney, you'll probably be given more leeway by the judges and clerks in juvenile court.

In custody cases in juvenile court, judges are often quicker to appoint Guardians *ad litem*. The Guardian *ad litem* (or GAL, as they are often known) is an attorney appointed by the court to represent the child's best interests. The Guardian *ad litem* will meet with you and your child's father, as well as the child before the final hearing, where she will give a final report recommending the custodial arrangement she thinks will be best. She, as an attorney, will also be able to question and cross examine witnesses, just like a regular attorney. You will likely have to pay for the GAL's involvement in the case, though – which can be in addition to paying your own attorney.

Keep in mind, as well, that anything that happens in the juvenile court is automatically appealable to the circuit court. In order to appeal, you (or your husband, if he's unhappy with the result) will have to note an appeal within ten days, and then it will automatically go up to the circuit court – where you'll have to do the whole thing over again.

This appeal is an appeal of right, meaning that you can use it no matter what happens. You can just appeal because you don't like the answer. That can be good, in the sense that you can try to represent yourself first without an attorney to see what happens, but it can also be bad in the sense that if you lose you have to follow the lower court's ruling until the circuit court has a chance to rule, and also that you'll have to have a full trial on custody twice.

Once custody and visitation are determined on an initial basis, it is also subject to modification. Whenever there has been a material change in circumstances, custody and visitation is subject to change. Those petitions for modification would take place in the juvenile court, but, again, you can appeal if you don't like the judge's verdict. Alternatively, you could take the decision out of the judge's hands, at any stage and in any court, if you or your husband were able to reach an agreement about how to handle custody and visitation.

Circuit Court

Circuit court is a higher court than juvenile court. In circuit court, you'll likely find that the clerks and judges are less friendly and helpful. They are also stricter about the procedural rules you must follow, and you may find yourself excluded from presenting evidence, questioning witnesses, and asking for specific relief to be granted if you don't follow them.

In circuit court, it's much, much more difficult to get around without an attorney. In fact, I really don't recommend it.

Circuit courts are less likely to appoint a GAL, too. Though it does happen, and with some frequency, they don't do it as quickly or as easily as in juvenile court.

Additionally, a circuit court ruling is more or less final – which is nice, and also scary. It's good to know you won't have to do it again just because your husband has sour grapes, but also that puts a lot of pressure on you, your attorney, and the evidence and witnesses you present at your circuit court custody trial.

You *can* appeal a ruling at circuit court, but it's not an appeal as a matter of right. You have to note that there was an error of law, as opposed to an error of fact, which is a fairly difficult thing to do. Appeals to the Court of Appeals are super rare – and exceedingly expensive.

Divestiture

One other thing you probably need to be aware of is divestiture. Since your case is also part of a divorce, and a divorce can't be resolved in juvenile court, one or the other of you has the option to divest.

What does that mean? Well, if a case has been filed in juvenile court for custody and visitation, the other spouse can, *at any point*, file a divorce in circuit court. This divests – essentially, removes – the case from the juvenile court's jurisdiction completely. The juvenile court judge can no longer decide the case and must hand it up to the circuit court.

Strategically, this can be a smart move to make. If it happens to you, though, and your husband divests the juvenile court of jurisdiction (particularly if he does it at the 99th hour, after your attorney has already spent a lot of time and energy preparing for the juvenile court hearing), it can be expensive and infuriating.

There's nothing I – or any other attorney – can do about it, though. Divestiture is a right, too. Because there's also a divorce, the case really is probably more appropriately earmarked for the circuit court.

Circuit court isn't bad, any more than any other court is bad. It's intimidating, for sure, especially if you've never been in court before, but it's also convenient (not to mention cost effective) to resolve custody and visitation alongside the other divorce-related issues. After all, if you resolve custody and visitation in juvenile court, it's still subject to appeal – and that doesn't get you anywhere as far as your divorce case is concerned.

What if mine is just a custody case, and not part of a divorce?

If your case is just a custody case, you won't have to worry about nearly as many procedural choices. Pure custody cases – where there is no underlying divorce – are handled in the juvenile court. So, that's the appropriate place to file. You'll still be subject to the same rules and conditions as if you had a divorce case but chose to file in juvenile court (meaning, essentially, that your case is appealable as a matter of right), but neither you nor your child's father will be able to divest the case to circuit court.

Do I need to hire a lawyer to represent me in my custody case?

We've already touched on this briefly, but it's an important question, and one that warrants its own discussion.

Typically speaking, juvenile court has a reputation for being more user friendly than the circuit court. There's also the whole appeal as a matter of right thing, which means that, should you get a result you don't like, you can always appeal to the circuit court.

Technically, in Virginia, you can represent yourself in a custody (or divorce) case in the juvenile or circuit court. In reality, though, that choice poses a lot of risks.

Although you could do it, if you wanted to, I would definitely recommend talking to an attorney first, whether or not you choose to hire them, to help you make that decision. Keep in mind: this is your children we're talking about.

I would never recommend that someone with a case in circuit court handle it themselves. Although juvenile court may be easier, you do still need to remember that these are court proceedings to be taken very, very seriously. Even if you appeal the ruling to the circuit court for a new trial, you'll have to follow the lower court's ruling in the meantime. That can mean starting a new school year or going through the holidays or summer vacation without yet having an opportunity to have the circuit court hear your petitions. Depending on how backed up the circuit court is, it can take months before you get a hearing date.

Certainly, if your case presents complicated issues – relocation, physical or sexual abuse, addiction, parental alienation, military deployments, special needs children, etc. – you'd be better off to have a lawyer in your corner. But, regardless, it's a good idea to at least talk to an attorney about your case and your likelihood of success. Remember: you don't have to hire an attorney just to talk to one and have the benefit of some sound, specific legal advice. My recommendation? Don't make a decision about representing yourself until you've had a chance to discuss your case in detail with an attorney, whether you find yourself in juvenile or circuit court.

How is child support calculated?

Child support is one of those refreshing areas of law where there are black and white, hard and fast answers. So long as we know what numbers – regarding your income and your child's father's income, daycare expenses, health care expenses, etc. – we can quickly and easily compute child support.

From that point, it doesn't matter whether your attorney runs the guidelines, his attorney runs the guidelines, or the judge runs the guidelines – the number that pops out of the formula will be the same. There are very few areas of law that provide the same clarity as child support, so it's good to be aware of and enjoy the straightforward nature of this particular part of family law.

What goes into a child support calculation?

As you're already aware, and we already briefly touched on, there are certain numbers that go into a child support calculation. Specifically, we use the income of both parents (which includes any spousal support or alimony you may be receiving as part of your separation and/or divorce), any support paid for children of other relationships, the amount paid each month in work related childcare, and health insurance premiums *for the children only*. We also enter in the number of children. Two children does not double the child support you would receive for one, but it does increase support the more children you share in common.

Since the numbers that go into this formula are different, the support you would receive (or the support he would pay) for different children from different relationships would be different, too. This isn't about being equal among different children, it's about using the resources of the parents to maximize the best interests of the children those two parents share in common.

Primary Physical versus Shared Physical Custody

It also matters what kind of physical custodial arrangement you share with your child's father. In a primary physical custody scenario where you have primary physical custody, you would receive the maximum amount of child support.

In a shared physical custody scenario, child support is based on a sliding scale. Depending on how many days you have the children in a calendar year, you'd receive more support. The more days he has, though, the less you receive. Shared custody can mean anything from 90 days with the noncustodial parent to an equal split of the year at 182.5 days, so it can make a difference for child support purposes.

To get an idea what the difference might mean, let's run a couple different guideline scenarios so you can see how it impacts support.

Let's take a husband who is earning $100,000, a Wife who earns $50,000, work related childcare expenses of $1000, and health insurance expenses of $100, paid by dad, for one child. In a primary physical custody scenario, that gives me a child support guideline calculation of $1453 per month. With two children, that goes up to $1848, so you can see that the addition of the second child only increases the monthly obligation by $395 a month. Of course, if there were additional work-related childcare expenses for that child, it would go up more – but I'm trying to keep things consistent so that you can see general trends.

Let's look now, using those same numbers, at shared physical custody, with dad having 90 days exactly. Assuming all the same numbers, guideline child support would be $1356. With two children, it's $1706.

If Mom and Dad split the year equally and share custody 50/50, it changes the numbers even more. With one child, shared 50/50, and all the same numbers included, child support is $923. For two children, its $1,062.

So, obviously, the custodial arrangement makes a huge difference in terms of the child support award.

Could I be the one who has to pay child support?

Yes, of course! Keep in mind that the examples I used above reflect a family where dad earns twice as much as mom. In the event that you are the one earning more, particularly in a shared custody situation, or a case where the child's father has primary physical custody, you would almost certainly have to pay child support.

I can't run every type of possible guideline here, so it's a good idea to consult with an attorney to get an idea of what guideline child support would look like in your case.

Could child support be $0?

Yes! I haven't had that actually happen, but it is theoretically possible, especially in a case where the parties have relatively equal incomes and share the child 50/50. In that kind of scenario, it wouldn't be that there's *no* support, it's just that the support would be considered covered by each party during the time they had the child in their care.

The theory here – and the theory behind child support being less in a shared custody arrangement – is that, the more time the child spends in your care, the greater your expenses related to caring for that child are going to be. That means more meals you have to feed them, more diapers you have to use, more clothes and other necessities you buy, etc. This isn't always the case, as you probably well know. I've heard *plenty* of stories about dads asking moms to send diapers for the kids, or keeping clothes and toys mom sends for visitation and refusing to send them back. In fact, I even had one case where the parents fought over their child's winter coat – mom refusing to send the child in it because dad wouldn't send it back, and dad refusing to take the child without the winter coat, since he wouldn't bring one to the visitation exchange.

Can I refuse to send items with the children for visitation – diapers, clothes, etc.?

You're not under any legal obligation to provide diapers for your child's father during his parenting time. However, you do still have to be mom. Also, if you have a strong preference for some things, you may want to include the specific items your child's father needs to meet that preference. If you prefer your kiddo wears Honest Company diapers, or your experience leads you to believe that Luvs give your child a diaper rash, well, you do the math.

I'd also send along any "tools" he might need – diaper cream or the hypoallergenic lotion that your child needs, especially if your child has an allergy or something like that which would mean that general or generic products just won't work. A dad is a dad and a mom is a mom, and each have their place – but you're only hurting the child by a stubborn refusal to provide items that would make your child's life easier or better during dad's parenting time.

With that being said, many children *do* have separate wardrobes at each parent's house. You are not required to provide all the things to him, or to make your entire house worth of items available. I think that for bigger ticket items, like bikes, it's probably best to share back and forth, but for smaller items, like bathing suits or summer shorts, it's fine to have doubles at each house. It's probably best to not be nasty about it if for no other reason than that your kids are watching– and, after all, your children can't go to visitation exchange naked. I have heard plenty of parents just return the children in the clothes they arrived in, so that no other clothes or items exchange hands.

He won't pay child support. What do I do?

Of course, you can ignore it and do nothing about it (that's also not to say that he'll immediately and easily agree in writing to pay the child support to which you – and by you, I really mean to say your children – are owed). There is, however, a quick and (relatively) easy way around that: you can file for support in the juvenile court.

The good news? Child support is retroactive back to the date you filed for support, so you won't lose out on any time before then.

The bad news? Well, you might have to go to court. And, besides that, it could bring related issues of custody and visitation to the forefront as well, which may not be super pleasant to deal with.

Still, the court will calculate and order support, and award it to be paid retroactively, which could mean that he starts out with a big arrearage to repay to you.

What if he refuses to pay court ordered child support?

Although it doesn't happen much, it does happen. In the event you find yourself in this type of situation, both the Division of Child Support Enforcement (DCSE) and the courts can help. If it's ordered, whether in an agreement (as long as it's entered by the court) or because a judge specifically ordered it at your hearing, he's legally required to do it, and faces penalties if he does not.

Ultimately, if he won't pay, he could face jail time, but we have other ways of getting child support from him, too. It's possible to set up a payroll deduction, or even to have his annual tax return garnished. Those aren't the first steps we would take, but later on down the line, we could. Lots of parents choose to have a direct deposit set up on child support, too, so that they don't have to actually remember to pay it.

My experience tells me that he may refuse to pay, but that's probably mostly an attempt to frustrate you. Since he likely won't want to face jail time or other possible repercussions, he ultimately will pay up – though he might not make it easy on you in the meantime.

Can I waive child support? Or reserve it to be determined at a later time?

Yes, of course. If you don't want to push the envelope, no one is going to make you. Not an attorney, not a judge, not DCSE, and certainly not your child's father.

We see this fairly often, especially in divorce cases. You can't get an agreement in place because he's that guy who thinks he can push you into not making him pay child support. And you can push him, but if you don't get a separation agreement in place, you'll have to file for divorce, and it'll be more expensive and messier, too.

Maybe, after you've weighed the cost/benefit of your course of action with your attorney, you decide to waive – or reserve – child support to be determined later. Without that scary child support number in there, he'll agree, and you can get your simple uncontested divorce and move on with life.

But you know something he doesn't know. You know that custody, visitation, and child support are all modifiable if there has been a material change in circumstances. There's really no such thing as a waiver of child support, though there is such thing as not putting a child support figure in your agreement. Even if your agreement says support is waived, it is actually reserved. And, if you *reserve* child support, you don't even need a change in circumstances! As soon as the ink is dry on that separation agreement, you can trot yourself down to the juvenile and domestic relations district court and you can file for child support.

The judge will calculate support, just like your attorney would do, and order that he must pay support according to the guidelines. He may be mad, but, hey – child support is the law!

What about extracurricular activities and summer camps? Will he be expected to pay a portion of those as well?

Technically, no. Although, if you reached an agreement on these points, you could hold him to it. The court, however, probably won't require that he pay extra.

These expenses are supposed to be included in guideline child support. I know, I know – those numbers aren't exactly generous as-is. How can you afford the extras on top of it all? Well, the court is super behind modern parenthood, and these figures just aren't included.

Upward and downward deviations in child support

Although you could argue for an upward deviation in support to encompass these expenses – which you could also do to reflect, say, car insurance, private school tuition, or additional expenses related to AP exams and college applications – that's just an *argument* you could make. You can present evidence of your expenses, and the judge can either grant or not grant the deviation. Your likelihood of success depends on your argument, the specific expenses involved, your child's father's income, the duration of the proposed increase, the judge, his mood, the particular day, etc. It's impossible to predict!

Keep in mind, though, that he could *also* argue for a downward deviation. Hey, it goes both ways! I have not seen many of these arguments be successful, but it is possible – the judge could grant it. I had a case like this not too long ago; a husband made an argument for a downward deviation because he recently had to move (he was in the Navy), and he had spent so much on his legal bills that he couldn't afford to pay so much in child support. The judge was furious (even pointed out that the Navy covered the costs of the move!), gave him a good scolding, and ordered support by the guidelines.

I think a good way of thinking about it isn't "how much do I have left to pay child support after I pay my bills?" but rather

"After I pay child support, how much do I have left to pay my bills?" Child support is a primary consideration.

What if my child has special needs and additional medical expenses? Does child support reflect those costs?

Well, not exactly. Guideline child support is what it is. But, again, you could argue for an upward deviation, depending on what your child needs.

Remember, though, that health insurance expenses are often a different category. One party pays for the healthcare costs for the children (which is included in the child support calculation, as we already discussed), and then unreimbursed medical expenses – that is, those costs that aren't covered by health insurance, like copays – are split pro rata by the parties. Pro rata means proportionally, based on your incomes. So, if he earns 60% of the income, he'll pay 60% of the medical expenses.

However, to the extent that your extra charges are *not* unreimbursed medical expenses, or not covered by health insurance, I would think those would make very good arguments for an upward deviation.

What about my new husband's income?

If you've remarried, and particularly if your new husband's income is higher than your child's father's income, your child's father is likely to be a little bit salty about it. I can't tell you how many times I've heard arguments that the child is deriving support from the stepfather, and so he needs to receive less child support from the father, or some sort of variation of that theme.

Child support is between biological or adoptive parents only. If either or both of you remarry or form another partnership, it has no impact on the child support that you both owe to the child. You'll share the guideline amount based on your income (and as offset by the other factors we discussed earlier – health insurance, child care, etc.). It doesn't matter whether your new husband is providing some level of support – which, let's face it, he probably is; none of that lessens your child's father's obligation to the child under the law.

Likewise, it doesn't matter if he remarries. It's only his income that goes into the formula to calculate the guideline; we don't combine his income with hers. She has no obligation to the child legally.

CHAPTER 3: Child Custody Orders and Modification

Courts have continuing jurisdiction to modify court orders pertaining to children. In Virginia, an initial determination of child custody can be made in the juvenile and domestic relations district court (which I will refer to as the juvenile court, but which is also sometimes referred to as the J&D court or JDR), or in the circuit court if child custody and visitation are being determined as part of a divorce proceeding. In either court, the judge can make a temporary, or *pendente lite*, child custody and visitation order while the trial is pending. Legally, this temporary custody determination is to create a stable situation for the child while the custody case is pending but has no effect on the outcome of the pending case. In reality, custody cases can drag on for months or even years, and the temporary order, to which the child becomes accustomed, can set a precedent which may be difficult to undo in the custody case. Typically, at the onset of a child custody and visitation case, the court will issue a temporary order, appoint a guardian *ad litem* for the child, require both parents to attempt mediation, require both parents to attend a class on co-parenting, and set a trial date. After trial, the court will enter a final custody and visitation order.

If your case is decided in the juvenile court, you have an automatic right to appeal to the circuit court, as long as you follow the procedure for noting an appeal within 10 days of entry of the order that you are appealing. The appeal to the circuit court is known as a *de novo appeal,* which essentially means that it is a "do over," and the case is treated as if the trial in the juvenile court never happened (although unless you are granted a stay of the juvenile court's order, you have to follow that order until a new order is entered in the circuit court). Once you have a final order in the circuit court, whether as a result of an appeal from the juvenile court to the circuit court or as a result of a custody determination made in a divorce case, you may file an appeal to the Virginia Court of Appeals within 30 days of entry of the circuit court order. The court of appeals will not consider any new evidence, but will look at the record from the trial in the lower court and read briefs and legal argument to determine whether the lower court erred in its application of the law or abused its discretion in making findings. Because trial judges have such broad discretion in making child custody and visitation determinations, it is rare for the court of appeals to reverse a finding of the trial court. In the event you wish to further appeal to the Virginia Supreme Court, you may ask the Virginia Supreme Court to hear your appeal. However, unless the issue that is the basis for your appeal is one that the court wishes to consider and make a ruling on, the court is unlikely to consider an appeal at the supreme court level in a child custody case.

Once you have your final custody and visitation order, either party may file for a modification of custody and/or visitation. In order to modify custody or visitation orders, the person wishing to modify the order must first prove that there has been a material change in circumstances since the time the last final order was entered, and then prove that the requested change in custody or visitation is in the child's best interest, using the child custody factors discussed in Chapter 2.

CHAPTER 4: Special Issues In Child Custody

Often, there are special issues in child custody cases which must be addressed. They may require the use of **expert witnesses**, who are people who have expertise in a particular area of knowledge, through education and/or training, and who can help to educate the court about an issue and provide an expert opinion. If you have a special issue in your case, it is very important that you address the issue thoroughly and educate the court about your issue so that it is not disregarded and so that the court does not make an uninformed decision regarding the issue. Additionally, when you do have special issues in your custody or visitation dispute, you should consider collaboration or mediation, which may allow you to more closely address the unique needs of your child and your family than the more "cookie cutter" approach to custody and visitation that the court may take. In this chapter, I will discuss some of the special issues which arise in child custody and visitation cases.

Adoption

Most of the time, adoption isn't a big part of what we do. In some cases, though, it can come up in certain ways. Most of the time, the question is whether a new stepparent can adopt a child from a previous relationship.

There are all sorts of interrelated issues: termination of parental rights, stepparent adoptions, name changes, etc., on and on. While typically we don't handle regular adoptions, from time to time it does happen as part of a larger custody case.

Termination of Parental Rights

Termination of parental rights happens when, legally, the court severs a parent's relationship with their child. In order for someone other than the biological parent to adopt a child, the parental rights would have to be terminated, or the parent would have to have died.

It's not easy, as you can probably imagine, to terminate parental rights – especially over that parent's objection. Even a total deadbeat dad is unlikely to find that his parental rights have been terminated. In general, when we see this happen, its after years and years of documented abuse or some similarly egregious conduct.

Before you say it – it's not *just* because the court supports the rights of biological parents to be involved in their kid's lives, no matter how many times they've shown that they don't deserve that consideration.

It's also a financial matter. A child support matter. A parent whose rights have been terminated has no child support obligation towards that child. So, even if, for example, mom drew up an agreement that dad signed giving up his rights to the child, chances are very, very good that the court would NOT honor it.

After all, if dad doesn't have to support the child, it falls on the state's shoulders. The state is already overburdened with the children in the foster care system, and simply can't take on extras for no reason. Certainly not just because dad doesn't want to pay child support anymore and mom is willing to take advantage of that. Two parents on the hook to provide support for that child is ideal in the eyes of the court.

Parental rights do get terminated, but it's usually after years and years of involvement in the court system, documented abuse, a CPS investigation, attempts at reunification, and so on. It's not an easy process, and doesn't often, if ever, happen by agreement.

Stepparent Adoptions

There are lots of types of adoptions, but the one we see most frequently is a stepparent adoption – where the biological parent's new spouse takes on responsibility for the child. This can happen both when the child's other parent is living, as well as when the child's other parent is deceased.

As you can probably imagine, it's fairly easy in the case that one of the child's parents has died. It's just a matter of filing the appropriate paperwork. When the child's parent is living, though – and especially when they oppose the adoption – things can get sticky.

"I want my new husband to adopt my child."

If you're remarried and your new husband is interested in adopting your child, that's wonderful! With that being said, though, it may not be so easy.

If your child's father objects, you can have a hearing on the issue, but chances are good that unless there's evidence of pretty significant abuse, a judge likely won't terminate his parental rights and allow adoption. Even if he's a deadbeat, it's a strong bar to overcome the preference for a biological parent.

It all comes down to the best interests of the child factors, and, generally speaking, the court feels that having both parents involved is in the child's best interests. Not only that, but the child probably won't lose contact with the stepparent over the refusal of the adoption – he's married to you now, after all, so even if dad IS a deadbeat and doesn't see the children, they'll likely still have the influence of stepdad.

"I want to adopt my stepchildren – but my husband and I have separated."

If you want to adopt your stepchildren, you'll be in the same boat as the woman I described in the first scenario who wants her new husband to adopt her child. A non-biological parent has a lot to overcome if the biological parent wants to stay involved, for whatever reason.

Another little wrinkle I've seen in a couple cases is where the mom wants to adopt the stepchildren even after she and her husband have separated. In fact, this has come up in cases I've worked on several times over the years.

It's easy to fall in love with children. If you've fallen in love with your stepchildren, even though you're no longer intending to stay with their father, you're not alone – but you're still in a really difficult position. It'll be virtually impossible to adopt if biological mom opposes it (after all, it'd be her you'd be legally replacing) *and* you're not married to (nor supported by) the child's biological father.

I've had the most success in these cases with visitation being delegated to the former stepmom. It doesn't always happen, of course; as a nonparent (more on this later), you have a very high bar to meet in order for the court to award you visitation, especially over a parent's (or, worse, both parent's!) objection. If he'll agree to delegate some of his visitation to you, though, that's likely your best bet.

Name Changes

It's tricky to change a child's name, too. Unless the child is 18, if you want to change his or her name, you'll have to demonstrate that actual harm would befall the child from failing to change his or her name. Basically, that the association with dad's name is harmful to the child's psyche.

That's hard to do! It's not impossible, but it's definitely not easy.

As always, it's a good idea to talk to an attorney if you're trying to take any one of these routes. It's going to be an incredibly fact-specific analysis, and you can provide details that will help ensure that you're receiving the best advice possible. While you probably already know that this will be a tricky thing to do, you'll want to talk to someone who can weigh the advantages and disadvantages of all the information for and against your case for you.

Breastfeeding

Breastfeeding can become an issue in custody and visitation cases, as you can probably imagine.

Breastfeeding in general is fairly controversial, but it may be safe to say that it's at its most controversial when it comes to custody and visitation. Sure, some people get pretty bent out of shape when breasts are used for their intended purpose in public locations, but Virginia law on that point is clear (specifically, you may lawfully breastfeed anywhere mom and baby are present). While the law is no guarantee that no one will ever make an inappropriate comment to you if you breastfeed in public, it is a guarantee that the disagreement will only go so far.

The science on the benefits of breastfeeding is clear, as well. The benefits extend for so long as both the mom and the baby are willing to continue the breastfeeding relationship. Not to get too scientific on you, but breastmilk enhances a baby's immune system, encourages intellectual development, helps regulate their digestive system, and helps foster appropriate emotional bonding and secure attachments between baby, mom, and others in baby's life. For mom, it reduces her risk of breast and ovarian cancer, helps her lose that baby weight, and reduces the risk of other diseases, like Type 2 diabetes.

But what does it mean when it comes to a custody and visitation case? Do judges always respect the importance of the breastfeeding relationship?

In a word, no.

That isn't to say that judges are always on one side or the other; judges, like the rest of us, vary dramatically in terms of their opinions. There are supportive judges, and there are not so supportive judges. It's kind of a mixed bag. And, in most cases, you can't control which judge happens to be assigned to your case, and you may not even know his or her opinions ahead of time.

Why does it matter what the judge thinks?

Well, it's hard to breastfeed without a custody and visitation schedule that's pretty heavy on mom's parenting time, which can have an impact on the amount of time that dad has with the child.

As children get older, breastfeeding sessions tend to spread out – but, still, the baby eats at least as frequently as we eat, and often much more than that. Newborns can nurse every 2 hours, or even cluster feed (feeding semi-continuously over a period of hours).

What kind of custody and vistitation arrangements work best for nursing moms?

It's a challenge to find a custody and visitation arrangement that'll work for nursing moms and still allow dads to develop the bond with their children. Obviously, mom needs to have the bulk of the time, which means that either dad visits with the child in the mom's home or at a mutually agreed upon alternate location, where mom is also present so that she can nurse the child. Alternatively, dad could take the child, but bring her back in order to nurse.

Overnights are also challenging for breastfeeding children because many nurse at night. In fact, it's not unusual for a child to wake during the night until age 2 (or sometimes even longer) – and a breastfed baby will likely want to nurse.

Why would a judge disagree with allowing a mom to breastfeed? It seems counterintuitive to me!

Despite all the benefits to mom and baby, some judges take a dim view of breastfeeding. Not because they don't view breastfeeding as important, but that breastfeeding isn't more important than dad's opportunity to build a relationship with the child.

Some judges have a narrow view of breastfeeding, believing that it should stop after a certain period, or that continuing breastfeeding past an arbitrary age means that mom is too "enmeshed" with her child, or, worse, that she's using it as a deliberate tactic to keep dad's time with the child to a minimum and hinder the development of a healthy attachment between dad and baby.

Not only that, but there are alternatives to breastfeeding. According to some judges, mom can just pump – and, to them, that's good enough. While it's true that a mom can pump and still be able to feed her child breastmilk, there's no question that the benefits aren't the same – and, even more alarmingly, that it may be difficult, without nursing, for the mother's breastmilk supply to be able to keep pace with demand.

Pumping mothers often have difficulty regulating and maintaining their supply, which can lead to early termination of the breastfeeding relationship.

There's also formula. I know, I know – it's not exactly ideal, especially if you are able and willing to breastfeed instead. Formula doesn't have anywhere near the same benefits to mom and baby as breastmilk, but many judges are of the opinion that formula is fine, especially if it means that then dad will have an opportunity to build a relationship with the child, too.

Keep in mind that this is a generational thing, too. Many judges are older and were babies at a time when breastfeeding wasn't in fashion. To them, formula was fine – after all, look how well they turned out! It's more popular now, but it's a relatively recent transition. For moms in the 60s, 70s, and 80s, breastfeeding wasn't nearly as popular as it is today.

How can I convince the judge that breastfeeding is critical in my case?

Like anything else, your case will be made or broken based on the evidence you introduce and what you can prove.

It's not enough to say that "breast is best" and leave it at that. If you are involved in custody and visitation litigation with a nursing infant or child, you will need to educate the court about a) the benefits of breastfeeding; b) the mechanics of breastfeeding (why you cannot simply pump a week's worth of breast milk and send your child off for a week); c) the role of breastfeeding in the child's forming attachments with both parents; and d) weaning (how and when it may occur, the possible repercussions of abrupt weaning to satisfy a court-ordered custody/visitation order). Ideally, you would need to have several expert witnesses to address each of these components of breastfeeding.

A pediatrician can address the physiological benefits of breastfeeding. The pediatrician may also be able to discuss the

American Academy of Pediatrics Policy Statement on Breastfeeding and the Use of Human Milk, which is very supportive of extended, on-demand nursing.

A lactation consultant can address the mechanics of breastfeeding, such as how let down occurs, the need for continuous physical contact between an infant and a mother in establishing breastfeeding, how long it is reasonable to expect that the child and mother can be separated and still maintain breastfeeding, the limitations of pumping breast milk. She could also address, to some extent, what could happen if the child is weaned too abruptly. The lactation consultant will probably be the least costly of the expert witnesses that you will use, but may well be the most important. The court is probably less familiar with the mechanical realities of nursing a child than the fact that breastfeeding is beneficial.

An attachment expert can address the role of breastfeeding in the child's formation of secure attachments, not only to his mother, but also to his father and to others. The attachment expert can also address the developmental benefits of breastfeeding beyond the time when the immunological and nutritional benefits become less important, and the possible repercussions of abrupt weaning. Finally, the attachment expert can discuss appropriate custody and visitation schedules for very young children, whether or not the court supports breastfeeding.

While using expert witnesses can become quite expensive, they may be necessary if you are in litigation and the court needs to be educated on important issues. For a very detailed discussion on the issue of breastfeeding in custody and visitation cases, see Kristen D. Hofheimer, *Breastfeeding as a Factor in Child Custody and Visitation Decisions*, 5 VA. J. SOC. POL'Y & L.433 (1998).

Grandparent and Other Non-Parent Visitation

It's a truth universally acknowledged that children are wonderful. Well, unless they're terrible, because sometimes that happens, too. But, regardless of how terrible they might be on any particular day, they're certainly loveable, and they wiggle their way into our hearts – and the hearts of lots of other people that they come in contact with – in about a million different ways.

When grandparents and other non-parents (like aunts, uncles, and stepparents) start to petition for custody and visitation, though, problems often follow. It happens fairly frequently in custody and visitation cases, with varying degrees of success.

In visitation cases

In many, many of these non-parent cases, I see petitions filed for visitation only. This typically happens in situations where one or both of the parents are trying to keep the children away from the grandparent (or other non-parent, but I'll use grandparent the rest of the way through this section, so as not to be confusing) – or, at least, the grandparent feels that this is what's happening. The grandparent wants more time with the child, so she turns to the court to petition for visitation.

A petition for visitation is *not* a petition for custody. In this example, grandma is not expecting to take custody over from a biological parent. So, although I can certainly understand how off putting this would feel, I want to reassure you that a petition for visitation is a different animal.

When you and your child's father agree: "Grandma can't have visitation!

Additionally, she will likely have some difficulty prevailing on her petition, especially if you and your child's father are united in your agreement that this particular grandparent (or set of grandparents, or other non-parent person) should not have time with the children.

We've talked over and over again about the "best interests of the child", including the ten factors that the judge must consider when determining whether a custody or visitation arrangement is in a child's best interests. In a grandparent or other non-parent case, though, "best interests of the child" does not govern. The grandparent must meet a higher standard than "best interests" and prove to the judge that "actual harm" would come to the child if visitation is not awarded. I probably don't need to tell you that's an incredibly difficult standard to meet.

It's not enough to say that, "oh, the child will be harmed because she won't have a relationship with me". That's not actual harm. The grandparent would have to show actual, specific, measurable harm that would befall the child.

If you and your child's father agree that this grandparent shouldn't have visitation with the child, the court will almost certainly respect that decision. Hey, you guys are the parents! It's up to you who you allow to be around your child.

That doesn't mean, of course, that the petitions can't be filed, or that the court won't investigate. And you may very well feel that it's unfair that this non-parent person can drag you into court, especially when you and your child's father likely have very good reasons why this person should be excluded from your child's life – or, at least, that contact should be limited, and that specific visitation should not be awarded. You'll have to see the petitions through, but, as the biological or adoptive parents, you and your child's father have the power.

When you and your child's father don't agree about grandma's involvement

Understandably, it's a little trickier when you and your child's father don't have an agreement about what the appropriate scope of grandma's involvement in the child's life should be.

Still, it's hard for grandma to get her own visitation specifically delegated to her by the court. We're still talking about the actual harm standard here.

Most of the time, in these cases, the judge will find that grandma can have time if dad (or the parent agreeing that this visitation should take place) will delegate a portion of his visitation to grandma. Grandma doesn't get her own, specific, unique visitation, but dad can give her some portion of his time with the children, if he wants.

In custody cases

If grandma can't even get visitation, it probably goes without saying that, in most normal cases, she can't get custody either.

Though she can file a petition, alleging that you or the child's father (or both) aren't fit and proper parents for the child, we're still talking about the actual harm standard in a case where mom and dad have custody and visitation with the child.

In those cases, grandparents (or other nonparents petitioning for custody and/or visitation) must meet a standard beyond the typical "best interests of the child" standard. They must show that actual harm – specific, certain, measurable harm – will befall the child because of their lack of involvement. It's really hard to do, and these grandparents often lose their cases.

But there are other types of grandparent and non-parent custody cases. Specifically, there are cases where mom and dad voluntarily gave up custody to a grandparent or other non-parent for a period of time, and then want it back.

Why would a parent give up custody?

Parents give up custody for all sorts of reasons, but the most common reason I see is drug or alcohol addiction.

It's hard to describe a typical scenario, because each situation is so completely different. But, often in these cases, the parent's addiction has reached a level that she feels she can't adequately care for the children. Instead of continuing to try to parent through the addiction, she takes some time out to get the help she needs to get sober again.

I've also seen it happen in cases where the parents are moving around a lot and don't have a stable home for the child. A mom might choose to have the children live with grandma for a period of time so that they can stay enrolled in one particular school system until the parent finds a more permanent arrangement.

There can be lots of reasons, but the impact is the same: giving up custody, even if it's intended to be temporary, can create a myriad of problems.

It happens a lot. In general, I think it's safe to say that it's always a bad idea to give someone else custody of your child, even if you intend that the arrangement will only be temporary. (In fact, in almost all of these cases, the situation was intended to only be temporary!) Whenever you voluntarily relinquish custody to someone else, you create a much, much more difficult climate for yourself in which to face a custody case later on down the line.

Before you sign over custody to anyone else, talk to an attorney about your choice, any alternatives you might have, and how to make your "temporary" arrangement as ironclad as possible. It may not be as easy as you think it should be to pick back up where you left off, especially if your child's new custodian opposes a return to the former custodial arrangement.

What happens if I sign over custody to a grandparent?

Once you've given custody to a grandparent, you're on equal footing with them in court. You've removed the "actual harm" standard, and instead have placed yourself on equal footing with the grandparent. Now, you must use the "best interests of the child" standard, which is much more egalitarian.

Grandma can now participate in the litigation the same as you. She can oppose your petitions for custody and visitation and argue for her own proposed custodial arrangement. If there's a Guardian *ad litem*, the GAL will consider the strengths and weaknesses of both of you in making a recommendation to the court.

If I gave up custody, will the judge hold it against me?

This is such a hard question to answer. I'm inclined to say "no," but I don't want you to think that means that you'll definitely get custody back. You may or may not.

A custody case isn't about mom or dad, or, in this case, mom, dad, and grandma. It's about the child involved, and what's in his or her best interests. Based on the fact that you gave up custody voluntarily, I think it's safe to assume that the judge will wonder whether you can give the child the stability and continuity she needs.

Sure, the judge understands that it's a good choice to not expose your child to your drug or alcohol addiction, but it doesn't necessarily follow that the judge will also feel that it's a good idea to return the child to your care immediately.

Other factors matter, too. The bond the child has developed with the grandparent, for example, and the ease with which you can continue to co-parent. If the child would have to move or switch schools, that's a consideration, as well. These cases are complicated, costly, and often very time consuming. There are a lot of factors involved, and it's a complicated weighing of advantages and disadvantages.

Will the judge take grandma's bad behavior into consideration?

The answer here is the same as the one above. It's really not so much a question of you, dad, or grandma, or your behavior and motivations. It is about the child and assessing what kind of custodial arrangement is in his or her best interests.

To the extent that grandma's bad behavior has an impact on the child, or an impact on the co-parenting relationship (which also impacts the child), her bad behavior would be taken into account.

So, too, would a lot of other factors: her health, for example. If she's old and somewhat infirm (hey, she is a grandma!) that can play in your favor, especially if, by comparison, you are young and healthy and able to keep up with the active needs of the child.

It's complicated. There are a lot of factors. Everything from this point forward depends on whether returning the child to your care or keeping the child with grandma is, in the judge's opinion, in the child's best interests.

Can I introduce evidence, witnesses, or experts to show that grandma having the child is not in her best interests?

Of course. This is now a custody case, just like any other. You can always introduce your evidence, bring your witnesses, or question your experts to show why the custodial arrangement you favor is in the child's best interests.

What's the hardest part of these grandparent custody cases?

The hardest part of a grandparent custody case is the fact that judges are often loath to disrupt the status quo. If the child is with grandma and doing well, it's hard to justify uprooting her yet again to place her back in mom's care.

The judge will look very carefully at the child, but particularly at her performance in school, her involvement with extracurricular activities, and the extent to which these things would change if a different custodial arrangement were ordered. For a child who is doing well and seems happy and adjusted, it may be an even steeper uphill battle.

Do I need an attorney for a grandparent custody case?

Almost certainly, yes. These cases are complicated, and often involve a lot of moving parts.

If your case starts in the juvenile court – as it likely will, as a modification of custody and visitation – keep in mind that you can appeal to the circuit court should it not end the way you wish it would. Still, when you're juggling evidence, witnesses, experts, Guardians *ad litem*, and all the custody factors, you'll want an attorney on your side.

Same-Sex Relationships

When it comes to custody cases where same sex relationships are an issue, things get complicated really, really quickly, mostly because there are all sorts of different types and categories of relationships that fall under this heading.

Not only that, but same sex relationships and how they're treated, especially as it relates to custody and visitation determinations, is currently in a period of flux throughout the entire United States. It's difficult to write to address these particular types of cases because so much is constantly changing – and just one new case could be a landmark decision that changes everything. That could happen in other areas of law, too, but it's less likely; so much less has been said and done as it relates to custody and visitation decisions.

All sorts of issues come into play in these types of cases, too – like reproductive technology (and, goodness gracious, do *those* cases present complicated issues quickly!). In this section, I'm going to talk about a number of issues in custody and visitation cases where same sex relationships are an issue. I'll cover both cases where the parties are (and have always been) same sex partners, and also cases where one party has left a heterosexual relationship for a homosexual one. We'll talk a little bit about reproductive technology as well, with the caveat that this category of law can change quickly (both in terms of the mindsets of judges, Guardians ad litem, and custody evaluators and in terms of specific statutory and judicial precedents) so, if you're facing a case like this, you'll want to talk to a lawyer one-on-one about the specific issues raised in your case as well as any potential outcomes.

I'll just come right out and say it: Virginia is conservative. And in Virginia, as in pretty much everywhere else, the law is slow to change. Although I do think we're definitely moving towards kinder, more tolerant policies when it comes to same sex custody and visitation cases.

What has the law been historically?

Maybe to understand where we're going, it's best to at least discuss where we've come from. The "old" standard in custody and visitation cases in same sex relationships was *Bottoms v. Virginia,* which was decided way, way back in 1995. In *Bottoms,* the court found that sodomy – conduct inherent in same sex relationships – was illegal, and so a mom engaged in that kind of activity was engaged in illegal activity. Not only that, but the court worried that the child would suffer from "social condemnation" from living in a household with lesbians.

In 2008 a similar issue presented itself in in *Miller-Jenkins v. Miller Jenkins.* Though it's more positive towards recognition of a same sex relationship, the court's decision was based instead on procedural rules rather than actual support of the substance of the case.

71

Of course, in the wake of the United States Supreme Court's landmark *Lawrence v. Texas* decision in 2003, sodomy is no longer illegal, so the rationale applied in *Bottoms* no longer applies. The stigma, too, is lessening all the time, so the whole "social condemnation" thing is more speculative now than before.

What's happening in same-sex custody and visitation cases now?

Well, since the Supreme Court's *Obergefell* case in 2015, gay marriage is legal throughout the United States, which has definitely led (understandably) to an increase in gay divorce cases, which translates to more gay custody cases, too.

In a sense, although this kind of recognition for same sex marriages is relatively new, these types of cases – where both parents are and have always been engaged in a homosexual relationship – are easier.

Custody and visitation cases where *both* parents are gay

When you have a custody and visitation case between two gay parents, it's harder for an anti-gay stereotype to enter into the equation. There's not a heterosexual parent there, also petitioning for custody. You just have two parents – whether they be two men or two women – so, really, all the court can do is fall back on those "best interests of the child" standards and apply them.

In these cases, the court's preference (if there even is one) for a heterosexual parent is largely irrelevant. It's not within the court's power to, say, put the child up for adoption into a heterosexual home just because the court doesn't like the fact that the parents are gay. Parental rights can't be terminated on this basis, either, and, anyway, that's not the kind of case we're talking about here. We're talking about a pure custody, visitation, and child support case (which may or may not be part of a larger divorce action) between two parents, who just so happen to be gay. A decision regarding custody would have to be made, and, in the sense that both parents are already admittedly gay, there's not much room for the nasty stereotypes and prejudices of yesteryear to come into play.

Reproductive Technology

Where it really gets tricky is where there are more complicated reproductive technology issues. It probably comes as no surprise that these issues come up – and frequently become even bigger issues than the matter of the gay relationship itself – more often in same sex cases.

The court has to define what a parent is, especially when there may be no actual biological ties between one (or both!) parents and the child in question. Advances in reproductive medicine have meant that all sorts of things are possible – the adoption of a donor embryo, or the use of a woman's own egg fertilized by donor sperm.

We see lots of gay couples do all sorts of things – like gestate one woman's egg in the other woman's body, or even alternate who carries donor embryos so that each partner has carried one of their children. These kinds of ties matter to the court.

Legal ties matter as well, like who was listed on the birth certificate.

Is a parent someone who has a biological tie to a child, or could it be someone who, though not biologically related, played a fundamental role in the upbringing of the child? Does parenthood require formal adoption? It's unclear.

What is clear, though, is that gay couples face these issues way more often than heterosexual couples.

What can be done to protect non-biological gay parent's rights to the children?

The easiest, most logical way to protect non-biological gay parent's rights would be to have the parents marry. A child born into a marriage is presumed to be the child of the parties to the marriage.

A formal step parent adoption is another option, but it is pretty clear that one of these steps should probably be taken in the event that both parents want to be equally recognized as having a role in the life of the child, especially if any future custody disputes arise.

This is a problem that heterosexual couples also face: when things are good, it seems unnecessary (or even inflammatory) to pursue various legal protections. After all, who is thinking about divorce? But, when things start to go south, it is important to have these kinds of legal details ironed out. It can help parties avoid huge legal issues later on.

Now, let's take a different side of the issue. Up to this point, we have talked about issues that gay parents face in custody and visitation cases, with specific emphasis on couples who have always been gay. I don't say "always" to ignite any kind of nature or nurture debate, but merely to illustrate that there are some differences between gay partners who had children together and divorced, and heterosexual couples where one parent subsequently engages in a same sex relationship (though these people, too, have likely "always" been gay, and I certainly mean no disrespect!), I am trying to draw a distinction between those people who had their own biological children with a different partner before their gay relationship began.

In the first type of case, the question is whether both parents are considered parents for the purposes of sharing a custody and visitation arrangement. In this second type of case, the issues are less about giving the gay stepparent any rights to the child and more about maintaining access to the children for the parent who is now engaged in a same sex relationship. It's important to make that distinction, because it does make a difference in custody and visitation cases.

Let's go back to the *Bottoms* case, because it's an example of this second type of case. In 1995, back when *Bottoms* was decided, the court found that the lesbian mother shouldn't have custody of the children because she was engaged in illegal conduct (specifically, sodomy) which rendered her unfit. Not only that, but the court worried that the children would suffer from "social condemnation" from living in a lesbian household.

To me, 1995 seems practically like the Stone Ages, especially as it relates to custody and visitation. So much has changed! While there's still the potential for prejudice on the basis of sexual orientation (I mean, just turn on the news), there's no question that things are better than they used to be. That doesn't mean that there isn't a long way to go until same sex couples receive the same protection under the laws of the Commonwealth as heterosexual couples, but – there's definitely improvement.

Although being a same sex couple who has had children by assisted reproductive technology has its difficulties, it's also difficult to be a mom from a formerly heterosexual relationship who is now in a same sex relationship. That fact will almost certainly be raised in court by your child's father and his attorney in an attempt to showcase to the court that, on the basis of your sexual orientation, you are somehow less fit to have custody.

Is the argument that, based on sexual orientation, a parent is somehow more or less fit to have custody effective?

Custody cases are always going to be based on the best interests of the child factors and how they interrelate. Opposing counsel will almost certainly try to use your sexual orientation as a reason for why you are somehow unfit, but he or she can only do so in the context of the custody factors.

How should I structure my case so that my sexual orientation doesn't take center stage? I'm a good mom and I've always been a good mom.

For your part, you and your attorney should make the case about everything *but* your sexual orientation. Obviously, there are lots of qualities about you as a mom that do make you a fit and proper custodian for the children, and that's where your focus should be. You may want to also bring in expert witnesses or others to testify – potentially the children's therapists, or even an expert who can testify that being raised in a gay household doesn't "turn" children gay. It seems like this is common knowledge, but in court it's always about the evidence and what you can prove – so even for things that seem basic to you or me, it can be helpful to have an expert there to get that specific evidence introduced.

In general, we've found that our cases like this have not suffered because of a particular party's sexual orientation. In general, trial court judges are much more interested in serving the children's best interests than they are in stereotyping or judging based on whether or not a mother (or a father) is in a same sex relationship post-divorce.

How do I show that I'm serving the child's best interests?

In this way, your case is likely no different from any other mom's case. We'll want to show that you're focused on the needs of the child, that you can adapt to them as the child grows and matures, that your physical and mental condition means that you're in good condition to physically care for a child, and that you're willing and able to promote the child's relationship with his or her other parent.

Co-parenting – the ability to work with your child's other parent to promote their best interests – increasingly factors into custody decisions. It's not just that you support the child's relationship with their other parent, it's that you cooperate in general with respect to a wide-ranging set of issues when it comes to the children. The court will be looking at your tone of voice in communications, the ease with which you make the children available to the other parent, your flexibility when it comes to difficult scheduling situations, and whether or not you share information from school and extracurricular activities, among other things. It wouldn't be a bad idea – regardless of whether the court has ordered it – for you to complete a co-parenting course before your custody case. It's kind of like driver improvement; it always reflects well on you for having done it, and it can also help you learn the verbiage that the court is looking for when it hears these types of cases.

I don't think that a judge would rule out a parent as a custodian simply because of their sexual orientation.

Attitudes are changing. Gay households are more visible and less unusual, and, even in Virginia, in some of the more conservative parts of the Commonwealth, we're seeing that reflected in the law.

There haven't been any landmark Virginia Supreme Court decisions on this particular issue yet, but, for the most part, we're finding that the lower courts are being much more egalitarian than ever.

Homeschooling

Many parents, throughout Virginia and throughout the country, choose to homeschool their children. Homeschooling is legal in every state, and in Virginia the requirements for compliance with the law are minimal. Homeschooling becomes an issue in custody and visitation cases when one parent wants the child to be homeschooled and the other does not.

When parents have joint legal custody, they are supposed to try to reach consensus on educational issues. When one parent has sole legal custody, that parent can make education decisions unilaterally. However, if the other parent feels that the custodial parent is making poor decisions for the child, she or he can petition the court for a change in legal custody, or even physical custody, upon a showing of a material change in circumstances since the last custody order.

If you are in a custody dispute and must defend your decision to homeschool your children, you will need to be able to show the court that your children are doing well academically, socially, and developmentally in the homeschool environment. You may wish to utilize an expert witness to talk about the benefits of homeschooling and/or about homeschooling and socialization. There are many homeschooling organizations available which may assist you in gathering information and identifying potential expert witnesses.

Academically: Standardized testing is a well-accepted method of measuring your children's academic progress. If your children succeed on standardized tests, it should not be difficult to show that homeschooling is working academically. If your method of homeschooling, or unschooling, is one in which standardized testing cannot adequately show how your children are learning, you may want to put together a portfolio or video displaying how you homeschool and what your children are learning. You may wish to have an educational assessment performed by an educational psychologist. Whatever method you choose, you will need to be able to show children's academic progress in your homeschool.

Socially: Many opponents of homeschooling cite socialization as their reason to object to homeschooling. There have been many studies which show that homeschooled children are socialized equally well or better than their public and private school peers. Dr. Susan McDowell has written a book in which she has reviewed the research on homeschooling and socialization. *See* Dr. Susan A. McDowell, *But What About Socialization* (Philodeus Press, 2004).

In order to address any concerns that the court may have about children's socialization in the homeschool environment, you will want to be able to show the court what activities, homeschool groups, field trips, etc. in which your children are involved and which give them an opportunity to interact with peers and engage with different types of people. You may also want to show a written schedule of your children's weekly or monthly activities and make a video or photo album showing your children engaged in activities with other children.

Developmentally: The court will want to know that your child's developmental needs are being met in the homeschool environment. Depending on your child's age, this may mean that your child is getting exercise and fresh air, that your child has a daily routine, or that he can shower and dress himself, do household chores, etc. You may want to prepare an exhibit that shows your child's routine, chores around the house, and any other matters that you determine are currently important to your child's development.

Abuse

Abuse is probably the most difficult child custody issue. Unfortunately, abusive relationships tend to cause the highest rate of custody and visitation litigation. If you have been a victim of domestic violence, or if you are a parent trying to protect your child from abuse, you must tread very carefully. Do not ever assume that you will get custody because the father was abusive to either you or your child. Most abuse is very difficult to prove, and you will likely be accused of trying to undermine your child's relationship with his father for reporting the abuse. If at all possible, consult with an attorney who has significant experience in family law and abuse issues before you do anything.

The following is a series of tips to assist protective mothers in navigating the world of the court system, addressing how to avoid the traps that your abusive former partner will set in order to try to make you look like the crazy or unstable person he wants others to believe you are.

Avoid the traps that make you look like you are the unstable parent:

1. <u>Forget Fair:</u> That's right, forget fair. Swallow the pill early and wholly. None of what is happening in your life is fair, and the court will not even the score. Never assume that the judge is going to hear your story and then stand up for you. You can be sure that your children's father (and his attorney) will tell a very different story to the judge, and the judge will not magically know which story is the truth. In the courtroom, it is not about truth, it is about evidence. Do not get caught up with each and every time something happens in your case that is not fair. Save your physical and emotional strength to focus on your strategy.

   Sometimes unfair can benefit you in the long run. Most batterers are narcissistic. Given enough rope, they often hang themselves.

   Making things right in the system is a different battle than protecting your children. Do not try to fight both battles at the same time – protect your children first. Protecting your children is more important than being right about anything. Even if you do not agree with the rules, sometimes you have to play by them in order to win. Suffer fools if your must, and chalk it up on the "puke meter."

2. <u>Be aware of the effects of Post-Traumatic Stress</u>

Disorder. Protective mothers often find themselves in the midst of custody litigation following their own escape from ongoing abuse and control at the hands of the abusive parent. Because of this, the protective mother is often suffering from Post-Traumatic Stress Disorder (PTSD) while she is dealing with attorneys, custody evaluators, and guardians *ad litem*, and when she is sitting in the courtroom. The very fact that she is suffering from Post-Traumatic Stress Disorder can play right into the theory of the universe that abusive parent wishes to promote.

Because of PTSD, a protective mother is often worn thin and frazzled; physically, emotionally, and cognitively disorganized. She is at the end of her rope and can appear to others to be crazy, just as the batterer repeatedly says she is. Because the batterer is so persistent, the protective mother has often exhausted her usual allies, including her family and friend, and has often been through a few attorneys before her case is through. She has insufficient financial, emotional, and sometimes legal support and appears to others to have few "believers."

A batterer has often conditioned his victim to appear as if she is overreacting. The abuse, even post-divorce litigation abuse, can be so subtle and insidious that its messages and effects are seen and felt only by the victim. They are inherent in the relationship. When the victim tries to point out the abusive tactics to persons outside the relationship, she appears to overreacting to very minor and/or reasonable action on the part of the abuser. When the abuser then states that the protective parent is hysterical and overreacts to everything, he is believed.

Because the protective parent has lost faith in a system which has failed to protect her child and has allowed the batterer to have ongoing opportunities to further abuse her through litigation, the protective parent often appears angry and frustrated at the court system. The people at the top of the very system which is the subject of her anger and frustration are now charged with evaluation the reasonableness of her anger.

In contrast to the post-traumatic protective parent, the batterer will always appear calm, friendly, and helpful.

3. <u>Watch out for land mines</u>. Your ex will set them and then point his finger at you when you stumble into them, accusing you of "Parental Alienation Syndrome," the creation of Dr. Richard Gardner, which has not been accepted by the American Psychological Association, is not based upon good science, but which rears its head over and over again in custody cases with abusers. An example of this is the "friendly parent trap." The abusive parent makes an unreasonable designed to catch you being an uncooperative co-parent. If you currently have physical custody, the father will ask for visitation over some period in which he knows that you have something special planned with your child, or he will ask for something that you know is not best for your child, like bringing your child back from visitation at an unreasonably late hour on a school night. If he currently has physical custody, he will ask you to forfeit an important visit or create a situation where it becomes terribly inconvenient for you to exercise your visit. He anticipates that you will react in an angry and uncooperative manner which he will use as an example in court of how you create interparental friction. How you react to these set ups is extremely important and should be discussed with your attorney before you give any response, whatsoever, to the set up. If you are put on the spot and asked for an immediate response, your response should be, calmly, "I need some time to think about whether or not that idea is what is best for our child(ren)." Discuss with your attorney whether it is a point on which you should give in (and show how exceedingly reasonable you are to his

capricious demands), or whether you should counter with a calm, "No, I do not think it would be best for our son to go to poker night at Hooters with you this Wednesday night, but he would love to go bowling after school on Wednesday, if you would like to take him." When you decline the unreasonable request, always make a reasonable counter offer, and do it in writing. His traps depend upon your having a strong emotional reaction to his actions. If you react calmly, from a position of strength, the traps will fail. You may need an expert witness to testify about the fact that "Parental Alienation Syndrome" is bad science and is not accepted within the scientific community.

4. <u>Take back the power.</u> The traumatic bonding which occurs between hostages and their keepers also occurs between abusers and their intimate partners. The abuser creates a dependence on him and becomes larger than life and omnipotent in the eyes of his partner or former partner. He can elicit emotions from his partner at will – empathy, anger, guilt (even when the partner is the one who has been wronged), and feelings of powerlessness.

It is helpful to understand how the batterer operates. He uses coercion, power, and control. He has a sense of entitlement with, and ownership of, his partner/former partner and children. He uses manipulations, set ups, and mind games. The abuser projects what he is and what he does onto the subjects of his abuse, and he actually sees himself as the victim. He is a master of minimization of his own bad behaviors, denial, and blame shifting. He will use gaslighting, a technique of manipulating his victim and her surroundings so that she begins to think that maybe he is right, maybe she is crazy. The abuser will do anything to wear down his partner's self-worth. He knows that he can elicit an emotionally charged reaction from her, and he depends upon this. You cannot, and the court cannot, change this pattern of manipulative behavior. Your awareness of it, coupled with your awareness of your own reactions to the behavior, can change the cycle. Remember, his scheme relies upon your reacting strongly and emotionally to his behavior.

5. Do the unexpected. Not responding the way an abuser anticipates takes away his power. If he pushes a hot button, respond with logic and emotional indifference. Go along with his ludicrous demand, or offer a reasonable alternative instead. He will become flustered. Practice being non-reactive. Rather than reacting, keep a fact log of the dates, times, and incidences of his immature and selfish behaviors. That way, rather than making you look crazy, his actions make him look unstable. He wants to keep you in a constant state of crisis. Remember, what is most immediate is often not the same as what is most important. Stay focused on your long-term strategy. Every action does not require a response.

6. An Abuser's biggest weapons are also his Achilles' heel. A batterer's inherent sense of entitlement and omnipotence can lead to carelessness. If he feels that he is above rules and court orders, give him some rope, rather than exhausting yourself in an effort to reign him in. He may just hang himself. Also, he is so accustomed to being able to manipulate your behavior that he will be lost if he is unable to.

    His calm, cool and collected demeanor – if you think about it – is completely inconsistent with someone who is listening to evidence that his child is acting out, disclosing abuse, etc. If he were not the perpetrator, he would normally have some emotional reaction to hearing these things and would want to find out if the child is being abused by anybody. He would want there to be investigations, and he would be cooperating with authorities.

7. Correct the context. If your child's father has abused

your child, once the abuse comes before the court, the abuser will file a petition for physical custody. He will then have turned the child abuse case into a child custody case. This changes all the underlying assumptions, clouds the abuse disclosure in suspicion, dilutes the issue of abuse, and changes the focus and treatment. You need to clarify every step of the way that the abuse is not a custody issue. The disclosure of abuse preceded the abuser's campaign for custody.

8. Educate the court. Expert witness testimony on domestic violence and on child sexual abuse is extremely important, and, in some cases, crucial. If the abuser presents evidence that he "passed" a psycho-sexual evaluation or a lie detector test, you may need an expert on rebuttal to explain why an incest perpetrator can "pass" such an evaluation and/or lie detector test. Make each witness' testimony fit together. Show that each of your actions was a reasonable reaction to the events as they took place. Show why your story makes more sense than his, why your reactions to disclosures of abuse make more sense than his reactions.

Relocation

Relocation with children, either out of the state where the other parent is living, or a significant distance within the same state, is very difficult to do, particularly in Virginia. In Virginia, the parent proposing the move has to prove that the move is in the best interest of the child, independent of any benefit that the proposed move may confer on the custodial parent. A parent who is attempting to relocate with a child should thoroughly research the area of the proposed move. She should be able to show pictures of the home to which she wishes to move, the neighborhood, the school that the child would attend, and any church, daycare, or other place of importance to the child after the move. She should be able to show the quality of life and education available to the child after the move. If the child is engaged in sports or other activities, the parent proposing the move should research the resources for those sports or activities in the place where she wants to move. Perhaps most importantly, the parent wishing to move should have a visitation proposal for the non-custodial parent which offers enough time so that the move does not significantly interfere with the relationship between the non-custodial parent and the child. This will probably mean that most of the summer and holiday vacation time is spent with the non-custodial parent. The custodial parent should also have a proposal for how transportation will work for visitation. This proposal will minimize the impact of the move on the non-custodial parent's ability to spend time with the child. The parent should also be able to show how the child will be able to spend time with extended family members and other important people in the child's life after the move. It is crucial that the parent wanting to move can identify and prove that the move will somehow independently benefit the child.

Relocation in Virginia Military Custody Cases

We've talked about relocation generally, and how difficult it is to "win" a relocation case in Virginia. It comes up all the time, as you can probably imagine, but it comes up especially often, and more emergently, in military divorce cases.

When it comes to relocation, the stakes are always particularly high because suddenly custody *does* become a win or lose proposition. Whereas in a normal custody case where mom and dad live relatively near to each other and custody can be shared on some sort of regular schedule, it often becomes increasingly difficult to keep both parents involved to the degree that the court (and the parents) would like when a relocation is involved.

More and more often, we see the courts relying on the importance of having both parents involved, and that involvement being one of the chief determinants of what, exactly, is in the children's best interests. It's less a question of one parent or the other being more important, and more a question of how to keep both parents involved to the greatest degree possible.

When we start talking about a relocation, we start talking about different types of schedules. Instead of week on/week off, 4-3-3-4, or even alternate weekends, we start talking about children spending larger chunks of time (potentially an entire summer or the majority of some of the longer major school holidays) in geographically disparate areas. Though shared custody on a week on/week off schedule is often distasteful, imagining losing an entire summer (or, worse, *every* summer!) isn't much more palatable.

But that's the thing about the military: there's often not much choice. And we have a fairly large contingent of military families in our area, to say the least, so most family law attorneys – and judges handling family law cases – have a lot of experience with military families and the unique challenges they face, particularly when someone is PCSing. Of course, there's a difference between a relocation, and how the court treats it, when you're the military spouse versus when you're the active duty military service member. Let's first address those differences, and then go into some of the finer points of what happens when a military service member PCSes or even deploys.

When you're the military spouse

Unfortunately, when you're the military spouse, you're not given any more latitude than a non-military person who wants to relocate.

If you have a choice when it comes to the relocation, your decision to relocate will likely be looked at fairly critically. As we've already discussed, as far as the court is concerned, one of the most important factors when it comes to deciding on a visitation schedule is the degree to which the children will be able to have a close and continuing relationship with both parents. If you're moving because of *your* choice, and it impacts the ability of the children to continue to have a relationship with their other parent, it will be looked at particularly critically by the court.

Can the court tell me that I can't move?

No, of course not! You're an adult, and you're free to move wherever you choose. But, unfortunately, that's only part of the issue here.

The court *can* tell you that, while you're free to relocate, you can't take the children with you. So, for most moms, the practical implication is that the court can pretty much say that you can't relocate.

What if I move anyway?

That's where it gets complicated. In general, I think it's always a good idea to consult with an attorney *before* you take any big steps, like going ahead and moving. Regardless of your choice, whether you consult with an attorney or not, and whether you decide to move or stay put, you should know that there can be some pretty unattractive consequences.

Sometimes, it's easier to ask for forgiveness than permission. If you've already relocated before your case comes before the judge the first time, then your relocation won't be considered a relocation. It's just the status quo.

If, on the other hand, you ask the court for permission to relocate, the court will often say no.

That's not always the case, though. Sometimes, trying to go ahead and move can be extremely damaging to your case. Lately, we've seen a number of cases where someone moves away, and the other party files emergency petitions with the court. An emergency petition can be heard ex parte (meaning, without you having notice or an opportunity to appear), and the judge can order that you and the children have to return to the Commonwealth. On at least one occasion, I heard of a local juvenile court judge calling a woman and leaving her a voicemail to tell her she had to return!

In these cases, the damage is pretty multi-faceted. Of course, there's the expense and inconvenience of moving that now has to be taken on twice – the move away, and the return. It can be damaging for children, in the sense that they're being uprooted again, which is probably confusing and a little scary. There's also the damage to your case, if the judge feels like your move was taken in bad faith in an attempt to keep dad out of the picture. However justified you may be, it can be hard to overcome that initial bad impression created by the emergency petition.

So, can you just move? Maybe. But it's probably a good idea to talk to an attorney before you take any drastic action, so that, whatever you decide, you can at least have a plan of action for how to deal with the potential consequences.

What if he PCS's? Do I have to stay here then? Do I have to follow him?

The good thing about being a military wife (or ex-wife) is that his orders will likely change before too long – unless, of course, he's nearing retirement age and plans to stay in Virginia indefinitely.

It's often better to just bide your time until he gets a permanent change of station, so that you'll be a little more free.

Generally speaking, you're stuck in Virginia for as long as he is. But no one can make you move to follow him wherever the military might send him, and no one will make you stay right here once he's gone.

Of course, where he goes will matter. If he's getting stationed in Northern Virginia or North Carolina, the judge probably won't let you relocate to California. But if he's stationed in Texas or Japan or California, you'll have a lot more freedom of movement. Either way, though, him moving will allow you a lot more latitude than you'd have otherwise.

It's never easy to be the military spouse, and it's even more difficult once you separate – especially if you have children in common and you'd prefer to raise them closer to your own family and support network. Moving them away from their father, though, will likely prove difficult, and that's something that you should be aware of.

When the Active Duty Military Servicemember Relocates

What happens in a Virginia custody case when HE relocates because of a permanent change of duty station?

For the active duty military parent, relocation is a bit different. We talked about it from a military spouse perspective, but, in general, that's regarded a bit differently by the courts. Where the parent has a choice in the relocation, it's regarded less favorably. The courts really place a lot of importance on children being able to maintain relationships with both parents, and a relocation makes that considerably more difficult. It makes all the normal custodial schedules much more difficult to navigate, too – whether we're talking about week on/week off custody, a 4-3-3-4 arrangement, or even alternating weekends, these things become difficult (or impossible!) if there's any real amount of geographical distance between mom and dad. But, in our area, judges understand the military. And if dad doesn't have a choice, he really doesn't have a choice.

Is it inconvenient for you? Yes, probably. But there are also some advantages, too.

If he relocates, can he "win" custody from me?

Probably not. His relocation won't hurt his case (at least, not like your willful relocation might hurt yours), but that doesn't mean he'll have a good argument for winning custody. If you want to stay put, you'll likely be able to, especially if he's deployable or works an inconsistent schedule. That will factor into a custody decision.

If he relocates, can I relocate?

It's helpful, for sure! I like the facts of the case better if you stay put, at least until you've won primary physical custody, but it's possible that you could relocate at the same time as him and still keep primary physical custody.

If you *both* relocate simultaneously, there is an argument to be made that, either way, it'll uproot the kids – so you and dad are more or less on even footing. Both mom and dad could potentially make an argument that they would be the better primary physical custodians, so that's just something to be aware of.

You'll also want to consider where his relocation may be. If he's relocating to North Carolina or somewhere else that's relatively close, it won't free you up to move anywhere in the country. To the extent possible, the judge will want to see that your children are able to establish and maintain a relationship with both parents.

It's always a good idea to talk to an attorney *before* you move, though, to get an idea of any possible issues you may run into beforehand.

What does custody and visitation look like if we relocate?

Custody and visitation changes completely when there's geographic distance between the parents, especially once the children reach school age.

Usually custody isn't so much a win or lose type situation as you might think; the judge just decides to what degree the parents will share custody. In these cases, though, someone usually has to "win" primary physical custody because of the school academic calendar. Kids can't go back and forth very freely once they're in school; they need to stay put for the majority of the school year so that they stay on track academically.

There are some significant advantages and disadvantages with this. For one thing, assuming you win custody, it gives you control over the better part of the year.

It also means that you'll have to contend with the kids being gone for larger chunks of school holidays and summer vacations – which can lead to complaints that you have to do all the work but have no chance to share in any of the fun. (And, let's be honest, that's a fair criticism.)

There's no "one size fits all" for these types of cases, so it may be difficult to negotiate an arrangement that works. Of course, if you go to court, you'll have little role in the decision-making process at all, and you'll have to deal with whatever the judge orders.

It won't be easy, and it will likely involve your children being gone for larger chunks of time than what you're used to, but it can be done – and, if relocation is important to you, it may be worth it.

What if he's deployed?

Deployment probably won't open you up to a relocation. After all, deployment is temporary, and, as far as the military is concerned, it doesn't change his permanent duty station.

It will give you more freedom, at least during the deployment, to move around, visit friends, and vacation freely. But it doesn't come without strings attached.

Make up time

When one parent is deployed, the other parent is often expected to offer make up time. Maybe not 100% of the time that he missed, but it wouldn't be inappropriate for dad to get a larger chunk of time both before and after his deployment to make up for some of the time he'll be spending away.

You should be prepared to be flexible for requests like this; my experience is that judges are sympathetic and do tend to honor these requests. It's not enough to complain that your schedule shouldn't always revolve around his. Though it's definitely inconvenient, especially in this context, it's probably a good idea to keep in mind that it does sometimes work in your favor as well. (And, hey, at least he'll be completely gone for 6-12 months!)

Delegation of Visitation

Likewise, the court is often sympathetic to requests from an active duty military servicemember to delegate his visitation to someone else during deployment.

He can't have both – make up time *and* delegation of visitation – but he can choose how he wants to allocate some of his time while he's deployed.

It may be that he wants to delegate his visitation to his parents, but it also happens sometimes that he wants to delegate to his new wife. This will be seriously considered by the court, especially if he and his new wife have children in common. If you think she's inappropriate, for whatever reason, you will have an opportunity to raise this concern in front of the court if you oppose it, but you'll have to have pretty good evidence to support your conclusion.

It's not easy, but where there's a will there's a way – and where there are children in common, there's often a very strong will!

That's not to say that this will be easy, or that you and your child's father will suddenly be of one mind when it comes to what's best for the kids (hey, I'm not unrealistic!) but sometimes necessity creates common ground.

Special Needs Children

Custody and visitation determinations for special needs children can be very difficult, especially when the parents are not in agreement as to the severity of the child's needs and the proper course of treatment or other methods of addressing the child's special needs. It may be necessary to have your child's specialist testify in court about your child's special needs. It may be necessary to have your child's physical therapist, speech therapist, or occupational therapist and special education teacher, as well as any other professionals with whom your child works, present to testify about your child's needs and the scheduling concerns which may affect custody and visitation. It may also be necessary to bring in an expert on your child's condition to talk about recommendations and prognoses. Finally, you may want to make a "day in the life" video to show the day-to-day realities of parenting a child with your child's special needs and how well you and your child work together to meet those needs.

Parental Alienation

One of the sharpest swords in a dad's arsenal when it comes to custody cases is often a parental alienation claim. It's an easy thing to claim, and it often creates a really tricky "he said, she said" situation that can make it hard to assess the truthfulness of anyone involved.

That's the problem with custody cases, isn't it? How do you refute something that he just seems to pick out of the air? And when it comes to parental alienation claims, it's typically *not* something that can be easily refuted or that you can prove without a doubt that you have not done. That's part of what makes it so challenging.

Even worse? Judges are really attuned to these types of cases and tend to take these types of allegations very seriously. But we're getting ahead of ourselves; let's take a step back, first, and talk about what parental alienation is, and then we'll talk a little bit about what to do about it, and how to combat an allegation like that.

What is parental alienation?

Parental alienation happens when one parent uses his or her influence over the children to damage the children's relationship with their other parent. In normal cases, this is usually just verbal. One parent says something about the other in front of the child, like, "Oh, daddy is just so irresponsible," or something like that. Obviously, though it's certainly better if you don't say anything negative about your child's other parent in front of the child, what we're typically talking about here is much more serious.

To the extent that a parent uses the child as a confidante to discuss the terms of the divorce or custody case, or to discuss all the ways that the other parent has wronged that parent in front of or with the child, it can be very damaging. It happens with children of all sorts of different ages. For younger ones, it can be harder to diagnose, given that it's harder for them to have the vocabulary to express that one parent's words have made them mistrustful of the other parent – but it can be profound and significant. It happens fairly often when parents have discussions around (though not necessarily *to*) their child, thinking that the child doesn't understand.

With older children, it can become a big issue very quickly, as the children's allegiances are pulled in a number of different competing directions.

To the extent that your communications, either to the children or around the children, have harmed their relationship with their other parent, you may be "guilty" of parental alienation. Even things like using the children as messengers between the parents (i.e., "Could you please tell daddy that...?") can be damaging and should be avoided.

Of course, it doesn't have to be true – and, in many cases, it's not. Sometimes it's as simple as dad making up an allegation in order to undermine you or to increase his chances of getting what he wants in court. In other cases, it's an easy way for him to save face as he realizes that his relationship with his children is profoundly changed by the choices he has made (say, for example, to move out, to not pay support, to get a new girlfriend, to fail to show up for visitation, etc.). Rather than accepting that his conduct has something to do with the way these relationships with his children have changed, it's easy to point the finger at his child's mother and say that it *must* be because she's talking badly about him to the children behind his back. That's the only explanation! (I'm being sarcastic here, obviously.)

What can you do about a claim of parental alienation?

Parental alienation is especially difficult because, oftentimes, the only witnesses are the children. I probably don't need to tell you that we don't really want to drag the children into court to testify. Not only would that typically equate to a missed day of school (something that the judge would *not* prefer to see), but the potential damaging impact of asking the child to do something like that – to testify against one parent or the other, or even to give the impression to the child that he or she can choose whether to live with his mom or dad – is just too great to risk.

Judges don't like children in their courtrooms. They try to avoid it at all costs. In fact, in all my years practicing, I can't think of a single time a child was asked to testify. I've had children sit in the waiting room (which I still prefer not to happen) while a case is happening, but I've never had one actually testify. Though I've heard it can happen, I've also never had a case where a child met privately with the judge and discussed the case. Frankly, as a mom myself, I'd do just about anything I could to avoid a child being thrown into the middle of the litigation in that manner. If I wouldn't want it to happen to my child, I wouldn't want it to happen to yours.

So, what do we do when the child is the only witness, but we can't call the child as a witness (and the child may or may not be credible as a witness anyway)?

Typically, the answer to a parental alienation claim is to appoint a Guardian *ad litem*. A Guardian *ad litem* is an attorney appointed to represent the children's interests to the court. A Guardian *ad litem* (or a GAL, as we sometimes refer to them) will meet with the child, do home studies, talk to the child's teachers, therapists, or doctors, and, ultimately, make a recommendation to the court. A GAL will interview both parents, too.

The GAL will talk to you and talk to dad as well. Though GALs are a mixed bag (just like any other group of people on the planet), a good one can help shoot down a parental alienation claim. Of course, it's not conclusive – it's not like just because one or the other of you performs really well for the GAL that the parental alienation absolutely, positively 100% is not happening – but it can go a long way towards convincing the judge.

What can I do to help show that GAL that I am not alienating my children from their father?

It's a tough situation to be in, but there are things you can do to help show that you support your child's relationship with their father. For one thing, speaking that way – as in, recognizing that your child's father plays an important role, and repeatedly telling the GAL that you want to do what you can to support their developing relationship – will go a long way. Of course, you have to back your words up with actions, too. Placing a photo of your child's father in the kid's rooms, being flexible when he asks for reasonable accommodations to be made to the visitation schedule, and speaking positively about your child's father in front of your children, can go a long way.

In every interaction with the GAL, you should show her that you're doing what it takes to support the children's relationships. It's not a bad idea to take a co-parenting class, whether or not the judge has ordered you to complete one, and to use the information that you learn there to help improve your relationship with your child's father. To the extent possible, share the information that you get from school, doctors, therapists, coaches, and other important people in the children's lives. Scan and share information, send screen shots of texts with information you think he needs to know, and give him the tools (i.e., login information to apps that allow him to stay informed about what's going on in the children's classes) to participate on his own. Things like school pictures, report cards, progress reports, school performances, and parent/teacher conferences should be shared.

You can even use a digital forum to share this information. We typically recommend OurFamilyWizard. It's an online platform that will allow you to share calendar information, upload important documents, and even chat. If your case is heavily litigated, the GAL and your attorneys can also have access to your forum. It's pretty cool, and it's a good way to ensure that all of your communication is in one easy-to-access place. (Also, since it's all written, it's good evidence for court, if we need it.)

If your child's father has accused you of parental alienation, you'll want to tread carefully. Even though it's a really common allegation, and disproving it can be difficult, you will need to adjust your behavior.

Even if you've never said a bad word about their dad in front of the kids ever in your entire life, knowing that he's making these allegations is a clear window into his frame of mind and the allegations he will make as your case heads towards a potential custody and visitation trial. Knowing what you know, you should use this information to adjust your behavior and your case strategy accordingly.

I think it's important that we take a moment to discuss 5 common mistakes in parental alienation cases, and what you can do to avoid making those mistakes.

Mistake #1: Saying, "I'm not doing that!" and ignoring his allegations.

It's easy to disregard something someone says when you know it isn't the truth. Some of that comes from the self-assurance of being a grown up, and not taking on more of someone else's bitterness or meanness than you need to. But when you're facing a custody case, regardless of whether you feel your actions are actually parental alienation, you'd be silly not to listen up.

He's giving you a lot of valuable insight into what he's thinking, and how he plans to litigate his case. He's telling you ahead of time a lot of the things that he plans to say about you. It's not nice things, of course, but it does give you a chance to either turn your act around or beef up your defense.

Ignoring it is one thing (to be sure, it'd be worse if you retaliated in kind), but it doesn't help move your case forward. If you know that's what he plans to say, work with an attorney to come up with a comprehensive strategy to address it.

Mistake #2: Communicating verbally with your child's father.

"He said, she said" allegations will always be tricky in custody cases, and it can come down to whether you or your child's father seem more believable.

If he's charming (or maybe even a narcissist), he may seem quite convincing. And if all you have to offer as evidence is your testimony about how your conversations have gone, that may not be nearly as convincing as you wish it would be.

If you aren't getting along, it's best to restrict your conversations, wherever possible, to a written medium. You'll need to tread carefully – it can be hard to tell the tone of a message when it's taken out of context if read in a courtroom – but at least it'll be some evidence of how the tenor of your conversations have gone. If you're saying nice things, like, "Sure, we can switch this weekend and next weekend, since you have duty," or "The kids would definitely enjoy dinner at Chick-fil-A, they'll be ready for you to pick them up around 5:30!" it can really help your case.

It could also help undermine some of the arguments that you're unreasonably withholding the kids. If he's asking for something and you have to say no – because you have something planned, for example, or because what he's asked for just isn't appropriate – you can do it in a way that shows your commitment to fostering the relationship without feeling like you have to say yes just to pacify him. "No, I don't think dinner at Hooters is a good idea," you could respond, "but maybe that pizza place in City Center? There's a concert tonight and you can take them for Sweet Frog after!" Or, "I'm so sorry, I wish we could switch weekends, but its my sister's wedding in New Jersey!" Having those records will help you remember as well as help ensure that your comments are taken in context (and not just "Oh, she wouldn't let me switch weekends last November when I had duty"), and help make sure the court can see how you speak to each other.

You can use OurFamilyWizard or even just regular old text and email. Any way you can document your exchanges will help!

Mistake #3: Complaining to the GAL about your child's father's behavior.

Repeat after me: The Guardian *ad litem* is NOT my friend. Say it again. Better yet, say it like 100 times.

The GAL is there to do a job. She's not on your team and she's not on your child's father's team. It's best to not treat her visits as a chance to dish on your ex, or to discuss all the problems that you've had with him recently.

Stay positive and focused on all the great things you're doing with you children. Remember those ten best interests of the child factors, and keep your observations centered primarily on what you're doing to help ensure that all ten of those factors are being met while the children are in your care.

Icing on the cake? Have a picture of your child's father in their bedroom when the GAL comes to visit.

Mistake #4: Not attending co-parenting classes.

It's kind of like driver improvement classes when you get a speeding ticket – though considerably more helpful.

Regardless of whether the judge has ordered that you complete co-parenting classes, it's a way to show the judge that you're really serious and committed to doing as good a job as possible. If the judge hasn't ordered it, not taking it won't hurt your case – but imagine the leg up it'll give you if your child's father hasn't even attempted co-parenting classes.

If absolutely nothing else, it'll give you an idea of the vocabulary courts want to hear. Make sure you're talking about co-parenting, about fostering relationships between both parents (and extended families, if applicable), and always refer to them as "our" children. It may be semantics, but you'd be surprised how important that can be when your case is in front of a judge.

Mistake #5: Getting angry and defensive.

Don't overreact. Though I understand your fear, I don't want you to act on it. Remember, strategic thinking is critical when parental alienation claims exist, and you'll want to be sure that you're thinking ahead to the hearing — and not just focusing on whatever he's saying about you today.

The worst thing you can do is to retaliate or to actually act in a way that suggests to the court that dad's allegations were on point. Stay calm and rational.

If you need help managing the situation, it's a good idea to engage an experienced attorney and perhaps even a therapist. This is a highly stressful situation that may not be easy for you to navigate. It's normal to lash out in fear, but you need to be thinking beyond that kind of behavior.

CHAPTER 5: Alternatives to Litigation

Mediation

Mediation, under the right circumstances, can produce a resolution to your custody and visitation dispute. This resolution may be more closely tailored to the specific needs of your child and your family than anything a judge can come up with. Mediation is also far less expensive than litigation. Finally, mediation can resolve a dispute in such a way that it does not completely destroy any chance of friendship or alliance between you and your child's other parent. These relationships will almost certainly be destroyed by an ugly custody battle.

Mediation is probably not appropriate if there has been physical, verbal, or emotional abuse in the relationship, or if your child's other parent is extremely controlling and you have any concern that you will not be able to stand up for yourself. In mediation, you do not have your own advocate. The mediator's job is not to make the outcome fair; it is to keep you focused on the issues and help facilitate communication so that you and the other parent can reach a resolution. The mediator is supposed to screen for cases wherein mediation would be inappropriate, but this process is not failsafe. If you think that mediation is appropriate for your situation, by all means give it a try. If it doesn't work, you can always litigate. You don't have to come out of mediation with an agreement if you choose to terminate mediation. I recommend choosing a psychologist who regularly works with children as a mediator for custody and

100

visitation matters. You can then draw on the mediator's expertise in coming up with solutions for your child.

Collaboration

Collaborative practice is a relatively new method of dispute resolution, and one that can serve parents and children well in the context of child custody. In collaborative practice, you and your child's father enter into an agreement with your team of professionals in which you commit to resolve your differences without taking one another to court or using threats to take one another to court. You agree that you are going to treat one another with respect and focus on your respective interests to come up with a resolution that best serves your particular family. The resolution is reached through a series of collaborative meetings with the professionals involved in the process. They take place in the office of one of the professionals, in an environment which is far less formal and far more comfortable than a court setting. There is no game-playing, trickery, or possibility of loopholes.

Your team of professionals includes your attorneys and, depending on the model of collaborative practice that your attorneys use, may also include a collaborative coach for each parent, a child specialist, and a financial specialist. The collaborative coach is a therapist who assists you through the collaborative process, both outside of the collaborative meetings, when emotionally charged issues arise, and during the collaborative meetings, when discussions become difficult for you, and you need a timeout or assistance communicating your thoughts and feelings. The child specialist is a child psychologist who may meet with your children, and who gives suggestions to help you reach a resolution geared to the particular developmental and emotional needs of your children. If you have financial issues that need to be addressed, you may use a financial specialist to review your finances and make suggestions. If you are able to use the collaborative process, you will likely end up with a parenting resolution which uniquely fits the needs and interests of your family. You will almost certainly end up with a better co-parenting relationship with your child's other parent than you would if you litigated or even mediated your dispute.

CHAPTER 6: Court 101

The Stepford Wife Makeover

Even though you shouldn't have to, and even while the world is falling down around you, looking like what the judge thinks a mother should look like will help you tremendously. This is the time to succumb to patriarchal ideals of motherhood. Change the world later. This makeover not only includes your wardrobe, but your mannerisms and the way that you communicate with the judge and other important people in your case.

The most superficial change that can affect the outcome of your case is your wardrobe. At this point in your life, you may have to borrow clothes from your friends or visit a high-end consignment shop, but your clothing and appearance in court is very important to your case. Even if money is not a problem, and your closet is full of designer business suits, you probably want to wear something a little more maternal than that. While a business suit may convey that you are a successful, contributing member of society, you want the judge picturing you at a PTA function or soccer game, not a board meeting.

A nice, tailored suit in something lighter and less lawyer-looking than black, navy, or pinstripe is always a good bet. A knee length skirt is more "motherly" than slacks. Yes, it is old fashioned, but remember, in some states, female attorney hopefuls are still not allowed to wear slacks while taking the bar exam. This is the climate in which you are functioning. A soft-colored blouse or sweater and low heels complete the soccer-mom-going-to-junior-league-luncheon look. If you have or can borrow a set of pearls (they can be fake a la Barbara Bush) and earrings, even better. Your hair should look neat, but not severe. Even though it sounds silly and has nothing to do with the merits of your case, the judge will be watching you throughout your case, and the way you look will form a large part of the judge's opinion of your credibility and ability to function as a mother.

Always be courteous and polite to everyone in the process. If someone needs to play bad cop, let that be your attorney. The clerk and the bailiff are as important as the judge. Judges often ask their clerks and bailiffs about the behavior of parties when the judge is not in the courtroom. Likewise, if you behave badly in front of the secretary or receptionist of an evaluator or Guardian *ad litem*, you can be sure it will have an impact on what kind of person that evaluator or guardian thinks you are. I know one Guardian *ad litem* who has a hidden camera in the reception area of her office in order to see how parents behave with their children in the waiting area when they think no one is looking.

The Guardian *ad litem*, custody evaluator, and other professionals have immense power in your case. Do not argue with them, even if they are wrong. Put your best foot forward. If they do something wrong or make a mistake, tell your attorney and let your attorney handle it. Remember, you must always be the good cop, your attorney can be the bad cop.

It is also important to remember that the opposing attorney is not always a bad person. You may certainly disagree with her or him, or correct her or him, but do not argue or make it a personal battle with the attorney. She or he may not be personally invested in the case. Also, she or he may have fallen for the batterer's story, in which the batterer is the victim. Remember, your ex is convincing. He managed to pull you in at one time.

Super Dads

"Super Dad" is a special kind of phenomenon that is unique to custody and visitation cases. In most families, while mom and dad are together, it's the mom who bears the brunt of the parenting responsibility. It's normally mom who drives the carpools, attends the parent teacher conferences, schedules all the doctor appointments, never forgets a birthday, runs out for poster board the night before the school project is due, and on and on and on. Both the physical and the emotional labor related to raising children is, in most families, well within the purview of the mother.

When a custody case begins, though, many moms find that things shift. A formerly uninvolved dad suddenly asks when the next doctor appointment is, or shows up at soccer practice unexpectedly. He suddenly has plans for what he'd like to do with the children on the weekend.

For an exhausted, overworked, and overstretched mom, the new involvement can be a welcome reprieve. After all, doing it all isn't easy! It can feel like a breath of fresh air that dad is suddenly doing all the things you always wanted him to do before but that seemed to naturally shift to your shoulders alone.

Either that, or the sudden shift from regular dad to Super Dad can feel threatening. Now that things aren't working, he wants to act like a family? Now that you've started to envision a different kind of future, he wants to step all over the responsibilities that are yours? If tensions are already escalated, this changing power and responsibility structure can make you feel extra suspicious and uncomfortable.

Why would a regular dad suddenly become Super Dad?

I don't mean to scare you, but, generally, a regular dad becomes Super Dad because his attorney has recommended that he take on a more active role.

There are a lot of related points here, and I'm going to touch on all of them. Let's start with the obvious.

Chances are, dad wants some parenting time. At this stage in the game, we don't know what his ultimate goal for custody and visitation looks like – whether he's fine with every other weekend, or whether he's going for straight 50/50 custody. I do think, though, it's safe to say that if he's suddenly taking on this role, it's because he has been advised to do so.

Is it bad? No, not necessarily. After all, it's good for the children, particularly in a time of upheaval, to feel reassured that both parents love them and plan to continue to be involved. Maybe even more involvement from dad is a positive byproduct of this separation; he no longer feels like you doing it for him is good enough, he has to take on a more active role himself in order to stay involved. That could be a good thing.

But still, a custody case is a custody case, and it's important to be strategic.

Why would my child's regular dad suddenly become Super Dad? What's in it for him?

Well, there are a lot of ways to look at things when a regular dad suddenly becomes Super Dad. It may be that this is a bid for custody.

Is he trying to take custody from me?

In general, custody isn't so much something that parents "win" or "lose", though it can feel that way.

In most cases, where we have two regular, generally good parents, the question is not whether mom or dad wins custody, but to what degree the parents will share custody. That doesn't necessarily mean "shared" custody (which is what happens when the noncustodial parent – the parent who has the children less – has 90 or more days with the child during a calendar year) but is just a reflection that two parents are needed here, and that the court will try to find a way that allows both to stay involved in a meaningful way that suits the children's best interests as defined by the statutory best interests of the child factors.

There is no preference for mom over dad or vice versa. Though that may have been a thing way back when, these days we generally find that the court's goal is including both parents to the greatest degree possible.

There is no such thing as "one size fits all" in a custody and visitation case, and there are about a million different ways that the days in a year can be allocated between two parents. Chances are probably pretty good that if he's acting like Super Dad, he does want the custody and visitation schedule to reflect some time with him as well.

It's also probably safe to assume that he's a little scared of paying child support. This can be another big reason why a regular dad becomes a Super Dad – if he's able to get a court order or an agreement giving him shared custody, his child support obligation will be less. Under a primary physical custody arrangement (where the non-custodial parent has 89 or fewer days in a calendar year), his child support obligation will be at the maximum level. Once you reach shared physical custody status, though, it's based on a sliding scale – the more days he has, the less his financial responsibility.

Without knowing more, it's difficult for me to say whether his primary motivation is just to get more time with the children or to lower his obligation to pay child support.

Can I waive child support to get the custody and visitation schedule I want?

Maybe! If paying child support is his fear, you may be able to offer a reduced amount of child support to induce him to sign an agreement.

Some moms also waive or even reserve child support in exchange for their preferred visitation schedule, though this is not always possible.

Keep in mind that anything related to custody and visitation – child support, custody, and visitation – is modifiable based on a material change in circumstances. So, if he has an attorney, his attorney will likely tell him that he could agree to this – but then you could also turn around and petition the court for a modification of child support later. (Likewise, he could also petition for a change to custody and visitation if you did that.)

If child support is reserved, you don't even need a change of circumstances. You could turn around and file a petition for child support in the juvenile court as soon as the ink is dry on your agreement. You'd get support according to the guidelines, too, because it's the law.

He may be willing to agree to this to keep his support obligation low, but, particularly if he has an attorney, he may see through this and prefer to try to keep his child support obligation low by getting as much parenting time as possible.

Is there anything else I can give up in order to keep custody with me primarily?

Beware of this. I get it: custody and visitation are literally the most important things for most moms, and there's not anything we wouldn't give up if only we could be assured that the we'd get primary physical custody.

The important thing to keep in mind is that custody, visitation, and child support are the only things that are modifiable. If yours is a divorce case as well, and you give up your right to something else (like spousal support, a piece of the retirement, or your share of the equity in the marital residence, for example), there's no going back to modify it later. So, you could agree to get primary physical custody, give up some super valuable asset, and he could *still* petition the court to modify custody later. You can't then go back and ask for the piece of retirement or whatever you gave up then in order to get custody.

Make sure that you don't put yourself in a bad financial position in order to keep custody. Custody is always modifiable, and, anyway, you have to ensure that you're able to support yourself if you want to be able to keep custody. It's never a good idea to give up something financial in order to keep custody and visitation with you.

What can I do if my child's dad becomes Super Dad? How can I make sure my case is strong too?

It's super important to think strategically when a regular dad becomes a Super Dad. It's easy to make mistakes, especially because you're probably feeling a little off kilter with this sudden change.

The most important thing to remember is that you shouldn't deny him access to the children just because he's suddenly encroaching on your territory. It's a tempting thing to do, but it's probably one of the things that could have the worst impact on your custody case overall – and it's playing right into your child's father's attorney's hands.

Remember custody factor number 6 (we sometimes call it the mom's downfall) – which is, essentially, the propensity of each parent to support the child's relationship with the other parent. If you're denying time or making an effort to keep your children's father away from your children, there could be serious repercussions later. You can do this to your mother in law; you can't do it to your child's father, especially not when there's a custody case looming on the horizon.

I know it's tricky, but you'll have to try to find a new balance. If he asks for something that you're not comfortable with, it's often a good idea to suggest an alternative. Maybe not wing night at Hooter's, but family night at Chick-fil-A? Maybe not this weekend camping, since you already planned to take the kids to Ocean Breeze, but next weekend might work better? Often, communicating in writing is helpful because then there'll be a written record. You don't ever want to appear as though you're just rejecting something out of hand, but rather that you're offering an alternative as a way to keep dad as involved as possible.

Keep in mind that his attorney is probably expecting you to say no. If you're the one keeping dad out, it won't reflect well on you. It could make you look controlling or like you're not really able to co-parent – those kinds of things can be reasons that an otherwise awesome mom might lose custody. You have to show that you can co-parent with your child's father, especially right now when things are up in the air.

If your child's father is suddenly Super Dad, it's a good idea to talk to an attorney about the specifics of your case and how to combat his behavior. Not all Super Dads are the same, so strategy can look a little different from one case to the next. With a plan in place, you can mount a good defense, and be sure to put yourself in as strong a position as possible in case your case winds up in front of a judge.

What to Expect

Trials follow a basic format. The attorney for the **moving party**, or the party who is asking the court to make a ruling, first gives an **opening argument**. The opening argument is a summary of what the party is asking for, and what the evidence is going to show to support the court ruling in that party's favor. The **responding party** will then give an opening argument, stating what that party is asking the court to do and setting forth what the evidence will show in support of that party's request. Next, the moving party puts on her **evidence** through witnesses and exhibits. The responding party then puts on his evidence though witnesses and exhibits. The moving party will then have the opportunity to put on any **rebuttal evidence** that the party may have, which answers or disproves the responding party's evidence. The responding party may then have an opportunity for **surrebuttal**, where he can put on evidence to respond to rebuttal evidence. Next, the attorney for the moving party will give a **closing argument**, tying together the evidence that has been presented by both sides into an argument to persuade the court to rule in her favor. The attorney for the responding party will then give a closing argument, arguing how the evidence that was presented supports the court's ruling in his favor. The moving party will then have a chance to briefly respond to the responding party's closing argument. Because the moving party has the **burden of proof**, meaning that it is her responsibility to prove to the court that the court should make a change from the status quo, she gets the last word. Either before or after closing arguments, the guardian *ad litem* will give an argument that includes her recommendations to the court, and what those recommendations are based upon. The judge may make a ruling at that time, or she may tell the parties that she wants to further consider the evidence and make a ruling, either orally or in writing, on another date.

Sometimes the format gets thrown off track a bit. A trial may be continued because somebody is ill or may start late because the judge's earlier docket runs overtime. Do not be surprised if you and your witnesses are stuck sitting around and waiting at the courthouse. Witnesses, especially experts, may be called out of turn in an effort to accommodate their availability.

Often, custody and visitation trials are not finished in one day, and you will need to find another date that the court and all attorneys have available to finish the trial. This date could be several months from the original date. Your attorney will be accustomed to these things happening, as they are normal occurrences for a trial lawyer. They may be stressful for you, but you should be prepared knowing that these things do happen. If you start with the expectation that your trial may not begin and end as planned, you are less likely to become frustrated if these things do happen.

Courtroom Etiquette

If you are allowed to take your cell phone into the courthouse, make sure that it is turned off when you go into the court room.

When the judge enters the room, or any time she stands up, everyone stands up.

Do not speak unless you are asked a question. Refer to the judge as Your Honor.

Stand up when you speak to the judge.

NEVER MAKE FACES IN COURT, I MEAN NEVER!

I cannot overemphasize this. You will hear ridiculous things in court. You will be made out to be a horrible person. Your ex will tell lies. His witnesses will tell lies. It doesn't matter. If your face is contorted and your eyes are rolling while these lies are being said about you, it will make the lies more convincing. If you keep a poker face while the lies are being told, the lies are far less credible. The judge sees you on the witness stand, but also watches your demeanor while the attorneys make their arguments, and the other witnesses testify. Many judges are convinced that they can see what is "really going on" in a case by watching the faces, gestures, and demeanor of the parties while the case is happening.

Likewise, if the opposing party or someone else is lying on the witness stand, do not say, "He's lying!" or begin gesticulating or scribbling notes to your attorney wildly. For one thing, if you and your attorney have prepared together sufficiently, your attorney will already know that the father is lying. Your attorney needs to be listening to what is being said on the witness stand in order to effectively cross-examine the witness. Furthermore, it makes you look like the crazy person that the witness has just finished saying that you are. If someone is lying, and you are not confident that your attorney is aware of the lie, calmly and quietly write a note and discreetly pass it to your attorney.

Remember, the judge does not have a crystal ball that reveals the truth to them. The outcome of your case does not depend on the truth, but on the evidence that is presented in court. Your presentation in court and your testimony are part of that evidence. Always tell the truth, but don't spill your guts. While it may be cathartic to open up the floodgates and let it all come gushing out, litigation is not the appropriate forum for that catharsis. You need to speak in such a way that the evaluators, guardian *ad litem,* and judge are ready, willing, and able to hear you.

First and foremost, tell the truth. There may be some parts of your story that do not cover you in glory. You are human. We all have done a thing or two that we would rather not have to talk about in a custody battle. Besides the fact that lying under oath is wrong and illegal, it is far better to appear to be a credible person than a liar. The truth, with explanation, is always better than a lie or half-truth.

When you are testifying, organize your thoughts before speaking. If you need a moment to gather your thoughts before you begin, it is absolutely fine to take a moment to do so before answering a question. When you are on the witness stand, make sure you are answering the question that is being asked. Do not lose the forest for the trees. Not every detail needs to be presented in court, and diluting the important points with superfluous details can detract from the evidence that will have the most profound impact on your outcome. Give facts and not conclusions. It is the province of the court to make conclusions. Your job is to present the facts in a way which leads the judge to reach the correct conclusion themselves.

Finally, remember that the judge's attention may drift. Give the important details but be focused and succinct.

When speaking with evaluators, guardians *ad litem*, and other potential witnesses, *do not assume* that you can trust people just because they are supposed to be helping you or your children. Talk to your attorney before speaking to anyone about your case. Do not attempt to publicize your case without first discussing it with your attorney. Remember that you are only guaranteed confidentiality when you are speaking to your attorney outside the presence of anyone except your attorney and her/his agents. You have no privilege of confidentiality with the guardian *ad litem*, your child's therapist, or an evaluator. Also, be aware of the possibility that you may be taped. In addition, there may be a tracking device on your vehicle, your house may be bugged, and there may be spy software on your computer. Paradoxically, it is important not to tell people other than your attorney if you think that you are being taped or spied upon, as it will make you sound paranoid.

Surviving Cross-Examination

When you testify, your attorney will ask you a series of open-ended questions. This is called **direct examination**. Your attorney cannot ask you "yes" or "no" questions, or **leading questions**, on direct examination. She will have to ask you who, what, where, when, why, and "what, if any..." questions. In response to these questions, you will tell your story. You should work with your attorney ahead of time so that you will know what questions to expect and so that your thoughts are organized in your head. That way, you will be more likely to maintain the judge's attention by presenting only relevant information in a cohesive manner.

After you give your direct testimony, the opposing attorney has the right to **cross-examine** you. The attorney can ask you about any subject matter brought up in direct examination and can do so by asking leading questions. This is the opposing attorney's opportunity to try to trip you up and fluster you. The three most important things that you can do to survive cross-examination are:

1) listen carefully, 2) only answer what you are asked, and 3) do not lose your temper.

Listen carefully: When the opposing attorney asks you a question, and you answer the question, you are presumed to be answering the question that is being asked. Often, cross-examination questions begin with "Isn't it true that..." You absolutely must make sure to listen to the words that the attorney uses before agreeing or admitting to what you are being asked. It is okay to take a moment to think about what was asked before you answer.

Only answer what you are being asked: If your attorney asks you if you know what time it is, what will you tell her? If you give her the time, you are answering too much. She asked you if you knew what time it was. The answer should be yes or no. It is the opposing attorney's job to elicit testimony from you on cross-examination. Do not do her job for her. She will probably be asking you yes or no questions, and most of your answers should just be yes or no. Sometimes, it is appropriate to clarify your answer or clarify a variation between the way the question was asked and your answer, but you do not want to spill your guts when answering cross-examination questions. If your attorney objects to a question that is asked, do not answer until the judge has decided whether or not you need to answer the question. After cross-examination, your attorney will have an opportunity to ask you more questions to clarify your testimony on cross-examination. This is called **redirect**. If your attorney thinks that one or more of your answers on cross-examination needs clarification or further explaining, she will ask you about that answer on redirect.

Do not lose your temper: The opposing attorney will likely try to fluster you or make you lose your temper during cross-examination. She will likely use a harsh tone with you, speak loudly, and be rude. You may see red, and your instinct will tell you to fight back by being nasty and sarcastic in your answers. Resist the urge. Custody cases are won or lost by a parent's demeanor on the witness stand. While the rest of the case may be he said/she said, the judge feels that she is getting a firsthand view of the "real truth" by watching the parents' behaviors for herself. *It is absolutely necessary that you stay calm.* And if you do so, it makes the attorney who is attacking you look bad, and it may make the judge sympathetic for you.

After you are cross-examined by the opposing attorney, and before your attorney has the opportunity to ask you questions on redirect, the guardian *ad litem* (if you have one) will have an opportunity to ask you questions. After those questions, the judge may ask you a few questions as well. Pay close attention to any questions that the judge asks you, as you can usually get a good idea of what the judge thinks is important in your case by the questions they ask. Try to answer the judge's questions as thoroughly and respectfully as possible.

CHAPTER 7: Working With An Attorney and Other Professionals In Your Case

Working With Your Attorney

A few words about your attorney: You absolutely must have an attorney who "gets it," who understands your situation and does not second guess the gravity of your case. Your attorney must comprehend what they are in for. Attorneys often hate difficult custody cases because they are always hard fought, they never seem to end, and the money almost always runs out before the case does. Even if your attorney has the biggest heart in the world, they have staff and overhead expenses to pay, not to mention that they are probably in business so that they can pay their own personal bills, and time working is time away from their own family. Make sure your attorney is up for the fight, and make sure your attorney is being paid. You have the right to expect your attorney to work and fight hard for you, and your attorney has the right to expect to be paid for their services. Also, you need to have someone in your corner other than your attorney. Having a friend, family member, or therapist to provide you emotional support is an absolute necessity. Your attorney will burn out too early if you rely on them as your main source of emotional support. Also, many really great attorneys are lousy at providing emotional support.

Teamwork

You should acknowledge that your case is more important to you than it is to your attorney. Even if your attorney has her heart and soul in your case, it is your life and your child. You and your attorney should be on the same page, even if that requires occasional meetings with your attorney just to check in and make sure you both agree and see the same things with the case. You should plan your communication in advance, or it may not happen as it should. Trial lawyers spend most of their time outside of the office, and it can be difficult to get them on the phone. Set a series of appointments with your attorney well before your trial date. If you are having a difficult time reaching your attorney by phone, call the office and schedule a telephone appointment. See if your question is one that can be answered by a paralegal. Also, faxes and e-mail can be more effective means of communication than telephone calls, but do not turn into the boy who cried wolf. If you fax your attorney daily, your faxes will not get the immediate attention that they receive if you only send them when there is an important, time-sensitive issue. If you feel that your attorney may not be on the same page as you, get the kinks worked out well before trial day.

If you become dissatisfied with your attorney, do not fire them impulsively. Make a consultation with one or more reputable attorneys to get a second opinion. Often, there are minor kinks in communication that can be resolved in a short meeting. If so, stay with your attorney. It will be far more expensive to bring a new attorney up to speed, and your new attorney may not become as invested in your case as your original attorney. Also, many judges see it as a weakness in a party's personality or case if that person has switched attorneys. If, however, you have lost faith in your attorney, hire a new attorney in whom you do have faith. You need to trust that your attorney is doing her best for you, and you need to be able to work together as a team. If you can't afford an attorney, read and re-read these tips until you have fully absorbed them, and do the best you can.

The Guardian *Ad Litem*

One of the things that we get the most questions about when it comes to custody cases is the Guardian *ad litem*. Specifically, what a Guardian *ad litem* (or a GAL) does, and, ultimately, the impact that a GAL's opinion can have on a custody case.

What is a Guardian *Ad Litem*?

Nothing strikes fear in the mind and soul of a mom more than the threat of a custody case – especially when dad is unreasonable, unwilling to compromise, or somehow an inappropriate caregiver.

It happens a lot. Even dads who were never formerly involved – or who did some terrible things – can petition the court for custody and visitation. Dads can even petition the court for visitation of a child who is a breastfeeding infant. Really, any dad, at any time, in any set of circumstances, can petition the court for custody and visitation.

That's…kind of how the system works. After all, it's not like you have the final say in what happens. It's not like he does, either, of course. But in cases where mom and dad clash, Virginia law says that the court can make a decision. The court uses the best interest of the child factors we already discussed to determine what kind of custody and visitation arrangement is most appropriate, and in July 2018 the law also changed to say that the judge must equally consider all types of physical custodial arrangements (primary, shared, and split physical custody, specifically) equally.

In a custody case, typically each parent has an attorney. That attorney presents their case, pokes holes in the other party's case, and generally does everything he or she can to describe a parenting arrangement that he or she believes is in a child's best interests that also promotes his or her child's interests.

Children – by definition – are minors. They don't typically go out and hire their own attorneys, the occasional Jodi Picolt bestseller notwithstanding. Mostly, children left out of the entire process, and mom and dad's lawyers are the ones making all the racket.

That's why, in many of these cases, a Guardian *ad litem* is appointed to represent the interests of the children to the court. A

Guardian *ad litem* (or GAL, as we often call them) is an attorney appointed to represent the child's best interest. Just like your attorney can conduct discovery, hold depositions, introduce evidence, question witnesses, and make opening and closing statements, so too can the Guardian ad litem. He or she is an attorney – just one who happens to be representing a party who (almost certainly, at least) isn't present.

What kinds of attorneys become Guardians *ad litem*?

Lots of attorneys become Guardians *ad litem*. Like every other kind of attorney, there are good Guardians ad litem and bad Guardians *ad litem*. That should probably come as no surprise.

But Guardians *ad litem* aren't therapists or experts in child development, though they do receive special training (and continue to receive special training for so long as they maintain their status as Guardians *ad litem*). They have standards to govern their conduct which set forth specific things that a Guardian *ad litem* is supposed to do – for example, talk with the child, conduct home visits, and so on.

At the end of the day, though, a GAL is a regular attorney who chose to take this kind of case.

Can we choose our Guardian *ad litem*?

Sometimes! Sometimes they are court appointed, but if your attorney and your child's father's attorney agree on a person to serve as Guardian *ad litem*, the judge will sometimes honor that specific request. Attorneys do often choose to select their own Guardians, if only to avoid getting someone they don't know and who may or may not do a good job. It also depends on what court is hearing your custody case, as the process in the Circuit Courts is different than the process in the Juvenile Courts.

We've almost all had horror stories with Guardians *ad litem* who are difficult to reach and don't do their work until the 99th hour – or even at all. But, still, removing a Guardian *ad litem* once they are appointed is virtually impossible, and virtually suicidal to attempt. (After all, do you *really* want a Guardian *ad litem* that you've tried to remove – especially if all or part of your argument has to do with telling a judge that he or she didn't do her job? – making a recommendation about whether or not you should have custody of your child? Didn't think so.)

It's almost always best to try to work with your attorney and your child's father's attorney to select someone who does a good job. You probably won't like him or her very much, anyway, but that's part of the job. One of our attorneys, Caitlin Walters, worked as a Guardian *ad litem* in her former life, and she always said that she wanted to make sure both parents didn't like her to avoid any allegations that she showed favoritism to one side or the other. Still, anxious, worried parents say that all the time. They even analyze how much time the Guardian spends talking to dad versus mom, or whatever. It's not easy to like someone with so much power over your ultimate outcome, is it? Especially when it almost always seems like the Guardian *ad litem* is a bit of a wild card.

How do I know what the Guardian *ad litem* will say?

One of the Guardian's responsibilities is preparing a report prior to the final hearing.

Until we get that report, which is supposed to be submitted five days before the hearing (but is often received on the eve of trial) we don't know exactly what he or she will recommend.

And it's powerful – in a lot of cases, judges rely heavily on Guardians *ad litem* to help them make decisions. After all, the judge only has an hour or two, tops, with all the parties – and can't really perform home visits, talk to teachers or therapists, or even speak candidly with the child. The judge is often the person in the room who knows the least about the case, and it's difficult for them to rule on custody and visitation without the Guardian *ad litem*'s perspective.

That's not to say that the judge always sides with the Guardian. But Guardians *are* very well respected, and very important contributors in these custody cases. So you should take your Guardian, if one is appointed, very seriously.

Who pays for this third attorney?

You do! You and your husband share the cost. It's one of the many, many reasons that custody cases are expensive. There are a lot of variables you can't control, and whether or not a Guardian ad litem is appointed is one of them.

Judges – I think, anyway – prefer Guardians to be appointed, especially in cases where there are complex issues. I actually prefer a Guardian to be appointed in many cases, mostly because I feel like my client is generally a better caregiver than the child's father is! I do, though, try to ensure that I can have at least a little bit of say in who is appointed, especially since there's a whole host of Guardians who don't do the world's most stellar job.

Cases in the juvenile court are a little more flexible with payment plans than in the circuit court, but, still – it's a third attorney that you'll have to pay for, if one is appointed.

Will a Guardian *ad litem* be involved in my case?

In a case where custody is litigated in court, there are at least two attorneys. Your attorney, who represents you – and has a duty to represent your cause zealously; and his attorney, who, of course, has the same obligations to your husband that your attorney does to you.

It doesn't matter whether your dad or your great uncle or your ex husband is footing the bill for your attorney, your attorney represents you and only you.

So, that means that no one is representing your child's interests to the court. And, in a custody case, where the standard is quite literally "the best interests of the child", well, that's kind of a problem. Right?

Because your attorney will argue that what you want is in the children's best interests, and your child's father's attorney will argue that what he wants is in the child's best interests. Hey, maybe you have a good argument. Maybe it's the truth. But there's no hiding the fact that your attorney works for YOU, and does not work for your child.

In fact, in all my years of experience, I rarely meet the children involved in my cases. In fact, I think there's a pretty good argument that me meeting a child (which would mean that the child is in my office and – potentially – aware of what's happening) is patently inappropriate. I always discourage clients from bringing their children (except maybe children under the age of a year) to appointments and, when they do, often ask that the children stay in the waiting area.

I like kids! I'm a mom, too! I really love children, actually. But it's not appropriate for a child to be aware of the proceedings, and, in fact, it can be bad for their physical and mental well being. I don't want opposing counsel to say that you brought your child to a meeting with me, effectively telling the child about the divorce and/or custody case, and that you aren't aware of or capable of serving the child's best interests! Eeeks! Definitely count me out on that one. So, anyway, suffice it to say: I rarely meet the children, and that's as it should be. After all, I don't represent them.

I represent women, and women only. Specifically, women in divorce and custody cases in Virginia.

That's where a Guardian *ad litem* comes in. A Guardian *ad litem* is an attorney appointed to represent the interests of the child or children.

Just like you and your child's father can hire attorneys, a Guardian *ad litem* is an attorney appointed to represent your child's best interest. That doesn't mean that your child will have to appear in court to testify as a witness, like you may very well have to do. In fact, we almost always keep children out of the courtroom entirely – it's not good for them. Occasionally (as in, very seldom), a child will meet with a judge, the Guardian, and a court reporter in camera (that is to say, in private, in his or her office) and discuss a case, but, again, that's super rare. It's very, very uncommon for a child to appear in court, and I've never had a case where I've called a child to testify, though I suppose it could happen.

A Guardian *ad litem* will testify for your child, both in the form of making a written explanation of his or her findings to the court, and also in the sense that, just like your attorney and your child's father's attorney, he or she can question witnesses, introduce evidence, and making opening and closing arguments at trial.

But will you have a Guardian *ad litem* in your case?

If there are issues beyond the normal – two loving, basically decent parents who both just want as much time as possible with the child – chances are good that you will have a GAL appointed. In cases where abuse is alleged, whether physical or sexual, or if there are substance abuse or mental health issues, a GAL will almost always be appointed. If there's a big issue – like a military deployment or a move to a different state – there may very well also be a GAL appointed.

I think courts lean to being more generous with GALs than less. Often, if one attorney makes a motion for a GAL, one will be appointed.

What is it like to work with a Guardian ad litem?

Guardians *ad litem* are scary. They're necessary, too, because in a lot of cases, they're really the only ones with the ability to look at both sides and make a recommendation to the judge. But...they make a recommendation to the judge! And, in my experience, their recommendations are generally regarded pretty seriously.

So, yeah, that's a little scary. Inviting someone you don't know into your life, for the specific (and unnerving) purpose of ultimately making a recommendation to the judge about how much time your child should get to spend with you. It sounds a little crazy, doesn't it? But in cases where mom and dad can't reach a resolution on their own, someone has to get involved and make a final determination. Obviously, it's really up to the judge what he or she decides to do, but the Guardian *ad litem* has a lot of leeway to convince the judge to agree with him or her. After all, the GAL has the time to interview both parents, as well as the kids, (something a judge is not able to do), so he or she has a really valuable perspective. He or she has also been involved for a relatively long period of time, compared with the judge and others who might come in contact with the case, and has the time to craft a legitimate opinion.

My experience is that most people welcome a GAL at first. They think, "Surely, when someone else sees what's going on, they'll see what I see, and support my position!" Sometimes, that happens – those are the best cases. But it doesn't always happen. And even in cases where the Guardian *ad litem* ultimately makes a recommendation for my client, it's not always a warm and fuzzy road to get to that point. My clients usually feel pretty acutely, from the beginning, that they're there to judge. That's not a nice feeling. Especially for moms who are already stressed out from the rigors of facing a custody case in the first place.

So, what can you do? Well, in one sense—not a whole lot. If the court decides or the attorneys recommend the appointment of a Guardian *ad litem*, it's probably going to be best to just roll with it. There's no sense wasting a lot of time and energy fighting it; if yours is a contested case, chances are good a Guardian *ad litem* will be involved. Rather than opposing the appointment of the Guardian *ad litem*, your energy would be better focused on how to impress and convince the GAL.

What do I need to know to work effectively with my Guardian *ad litem*?

1. Learn about Virginia custody cases

   I'm not suggesting you enroll in law school or anything crazy, but to the extent that you can learn about custody cases, you should. Reading this custody book and considering attending our custody seminar, Custody Bootcamp for Moms (which you can do for free as a Hofheimer Family Law client!) are both great ways to learn more about how custody case work in Virginia.

   The more you know, the better prepared you can be for what's to come – including what the GAL will be looking for, and what he or she will expect from you.

2. Learn about the role of the GAL

   There's a whole cast of characters in custody cases, and the more you know about who each person is and what their role will be in the ultimate determination of custody, the better! This is particularly helpful with the role of the GAL, as there are things a GAL can, and honestly should, do that can be surprising. I frequently will receive emails or calls from my clients saying "the

Child Custody Survival Guide

GAL showed up at my house unannounced – can they do that?" or "the GAL went to my child's school and spoke to my child without telling me – can they do that?" My answer – yes, and sometimes they should! So understanding their role from the beginning can help cut down on a lot of anxiety, and allow you to continue to focus on being the best mom you can be.

BEWARE! Your Guardian *ad litem* has tremendous power, and it's important that you know and understand this ahead of time – before you make any missteps that could hurt your case. The biggest thing to remember? He or she is not your friend, and wasn't appointed to hold your hand through the case. Don't dump all of your complaints about your child's father on the Guardian *ad litem*, show how you're the most capable of focusing on the child's best interests.

3. Be familiar with Virginia's best interests of the child factors.

In Virginia, judges have to use the best interests of the child factors to make decisions in custody and visitation cases. The more you know and understand about these factors, the better prepared you can be to talk with the Guardian *ad litem* as your case progresses.

4. Be careful what you put in writing!

The GAL will be able to see most everything you write. They will see the discovery, and you can bet that if you say something nasty to your husband in an email or text message, your husband will share it, and you'll look just as bad as if you had said whatever you said to the GAL directly.

It doesn't matter whether what you said is reasonable under the circumstances; if you look like you're just as bad as he is, you're doing him a favor. If you want your case to be as strong as possible, make sure that you represent yourself well in writing, even when you're just talking to your child's father. Even if he is a jerk. Let *him* be a jerk – you don't fall into that trap yourself.

125

Ask yourself before you say anything, "how would it sound if just this text message/email were read aloud in court, without any of his messages to provide context? Would I look heinous?" If the answer is "yes", then don't say it.

Do I want a Guardian *ad litem* appointed?

A Guardian *ad litem* is an attorney appointed on behalf of a child in a custody case. We really don't bring kids to court to testify; there won't be a moment where the child has to tell the court whether he'd prefer to live with mom or dad. That just doesn't happen.

But, of course, in a custody case, the prominent parties are typically mom and dad, and their respective lawyers. Their lawyers will, obviously, argue *their* respective points. But where does that whole "best interests of the child" standard that you've heard so much about come in?

Well, it's with the Guardian *ad litem*. Though a child isn't officially old enough to have a preference until he or she has turned 18, it is through the Guardian *ad litem* that information related to the children will get in. In some cases, the GAL will specifically tell the court what the child's preference is (though this is not always the case), but in all cases the Guardian *ad litem* will make a specific recommendation to the court regarding what custody and visitation arrangement is, in his or her opinion, in the best interests of the child.

So, needless to say, the Guardian *ad litem* is a really important person in a custody case.

But do you want a Guardian *ad litem* in your case?

It's a good question. In a lot of cases, there's not a lot of choice. Judges like GALs, and often appoint them, especially if one side or the other made a motion requesting that one be appointed. You can see the judge's point of view: at least, with a GAL, there's one other person in the courtroom who is looking out for the child and can, at least presumably, give the judge a less biased view of the facts.

It's risky, though. A Guardian *ad litem* can be a bit of a wild card and if there's anywhere in the world there's not that much room for a wild card, it's in a custody and visitation case. It's scary to think that someone who is a virtual stranger to you would have the kind of power that would allow him to make a recommendation to a judge about what kind of custody and visitation arrangement is appropriate in your case.

There are a lot of things about custody and visitation cases that are probably pretty tough pills for parents to swallow, and this is one of them. But there's also no denying that having a GAL on your side can be one of the most powerful indicators of success in a custody and visitation case.

So, do you want one?

Am I beating a dead horse here? Maybe! And, anyway, you may not have much choice. In an ideal world, you'd be able to pick who you wanted as a GAL and, also, whether or not you even wanted a GAL appointed at all. In many cases, especially where both parties attorneys agree about needing a GAL, the attorneys help their clients to pick an appropriate person to serve as GAL. If you have to make a motion in court, you may end up with whoever the judge appoints – which may just be whoever is present in the courtroom at the time. Attorneys who can be court appointed are often found in the courtroom, waiting to get appointed to cases – so that can happen. If it were my case, though, I'd prefer to have some say in who was appointed. Like every other kind of people, there are good and bad GALs.

Can I fight the appointment of a GAL?

Yes, of course. If your husband's attorney makes a motion, you can oppose it. It'll be up to the judge, though, and I think you're probably not all that likely to be successful. Again, judges like having someone else there to help make a decision.

And, unlike petitioning for removal of a GAL later, I don't think it makes you look bad to oppose the appointment of the GAL initially, especially if you cite specific legitimate concerns (like, perhaps, the cost of it, or the fact that your child's father is trying to use it to take advantage of you, since you're the lesser earner of the two of you).

If, though, one is appointed anyway, you'll want to get on board quick. There's not very much you can do once one is appointed, and it's better to redirect your energy towards making sure that you make a good impression, and convince the Guardian *ad litem* of your position.

What can I do to make a good impression on my GAL?

Now *that's* a good question! It's far better to be proactive than to be the ostrich burying your head in the sand. Chances are good a GAL will get appointed in a custody case, and your efforts are far better spent trying to plan how to make a good impression.

Most GALs will start their representation with a questionnaire, which you should fill out promptly. If you have an attorney, your attorney should help review your answers before they're submitted, too.

Focus on how you meet the requirements of the best interests of the child factors, rather than detailing the ways your child's father falls short. In fact, it's probably a better idea to avoid criticizing your child's father in general and instead allow your GAL a chance to make up his or her own mind.

Be transparent, but don't overshare. If you have questions, talk to your attorney about how to handle specific situations.

Be realistic. The information that you share with the GAL is very important and will be relied upon as they make their recommendation. However, how you share that information is just as important to the GAL. We all have our strengths and weaknesses, and pretending otherwise in a custody case will not serve you well! So when working with a GAL in your custody case, you will want to really consider your weaknesses as a parent and the father's strengths as a parent. If you have an attorney, your attorney should help figure out the best way to approach this type of question with the GAL — again, you want to be transparent but not overshare!

The GAL will likely perform a home visit and will also interview the child (assuming the child is old enough to participate in this conversation). You should be prepared for this.

If your case is serious enough to have a Guardian *ad litem* involved, it's serious enough that you should have an attorney advocating for you. It's difficult to navigate the tricky waters associated with working with a GAL, and it's extremely helpful to have an attorney there to coach you through the process. Getting information about what's involved and how it works is good, but having someone on your side who can help you fill out the questionnaire, prepare for the home visit, and manage communications between you and your child's father while your case is pending is often invaluable.

Remember, too, that if your case is in juvenile court and you appeal to circuit court, your GAL will come with you. Not only that, but if you petition for a modification later, it is almost certain that the same GAL will be re-appointed again, barring that GAL's relocation, retirement, maternity leave, or other extenuating circumstance. These relationships with the Guardian can be for a very long time, and you'd be wise to make sure to get it off on the right foot. Remember: even if the GAL isn't your favorite person today, that's no reason to burn a bridge tomorrow.

Custody Evaluators and Other Forensic Evaluators

Speak with your attorney before meeting with custody evaluators or other forensic evaluators. Much like with the guardian *ad litem*, you do not have confidentiality with evaluators. Also, you must use the same finesse that you used with the GAL to relay your concerns about the other parent without bashing him. Evaluators are very much on the lookout for a parent who seems vindictive or overly negative about the other parent. Finally, if you have concerns about the way the evaluator is doing his job, address them with your attorney, not directly with the evaluator.

CHAPTER 8: 10 Tips for Representing Yourself in Court

1. Most of the work in a trial is done before you ever go to court. You must be proactive. Talk to everyone involved after being advised by your attorney. Evaluators, guardians *ad litem*, social workers, and therapists will have mostly formed an opinion before the hearing. You must be involved in the formation of these opinions.

2. Your conduct in the pre-trial phase is crucial. You are living under a microscope at this point in your life. Assume everything you do or say is known or knowable to your child's other parent and his attorney.

3. Discovery is a tool that attorneys use to find out facts, along with the opposing party's theory of the case and trial strategy. Extensive discovery is absolutely necessary in difficult custody cases. Dig! Dig! Dig! The truth is out there. Do not forget cell phone records; they can be very helpful. Plot every fact that you find out on your timeline of events. Connect the dots. The extensive quantity of relevant facts in difficult custody cases must be organized and digested well before trial.

4. File appropriate pretrial motions. If the other side has disclosed in discovery that they intend to introduce evidence which may be inadmissible, pretrial motions can narrow the issues and exclude evidences which should not be allowed. Trials can be won or lost on

pretrial motions.

5. Your courtroom demeanor is crucial. Judges often see *pro se* **litigants** (people who represent themselves in court) behaving outrageously. Of course you are more impassioned about your own case than any attorney could be, but you must be organized, logical, and not overly emotional if you want to be taken seriously by the judge. At the same time, you want to be yourself and not appear to be trying to be Perry Mason.

Make sure there is a court reporter at your trial. If there is an attorney on the other side of the case, call his office and find out if he has hired a court reporter. If not, call one yourself and arrange to have a court reporter appear for your trial. You can very easily do a quick Google search for court reporters. It is important to have a court reporter for several reasons. First, if you want to appeal your case, you will have to have a record of the evidence that was presented in court. Second, as a *pro se* litigant, you may get bulldozed without a court reporter taking down everything that is said by the other attorney, the guardian *ad litem*, and the judge. Third, if someone lies on the witness stand, you will have proof. Finally, if you disagree over whether a proposed written order accurately reflects what the judge ruled, you can simply order the judge's ruling to be transcribed, and you will have it in black and white.

Put together your evidence before you go to court. You know the story that you want to tell. Find witnesses who have firsthand knowledge (they observed it themselves) of events and determine what testimony you want to elicit from each witness. Also, determine what exhibits each witness can authenticate (the teacher can talk about notes that she sent home, the pediatrician can talk about medical records written by him, etc.). Put together a trial notebook that has an outline of your opening argument, your witnesses in the order that you can call them, the witnesses that you think the father will call, and your closing argument. Make a tab for each witness and put in the questions that you plan to ask the witness. For each exhibit that you plan to introduce, make three copies: one for the opposing party, one for the guardian *ad litem*, and one for yourself. You will give the original to the judge. Put your exhibits and copies under the tab for the witness that you plan to use to introduce the exhibit.

To introduce an exhibit, you will need to hand a copy to the guardian *ad litem* and the opposing attorney. You will then want to show the exhibit to the witness. You will need to ask the judge's permission to approach the witness before you walk up to the witness. You will then ask the witness to identify the document. You must then ask the judge for permission to approach the bench to hand the exhibit to the judge. The judge may instead have the bailiff take the exhibit to the judge. You will then ask the court to mark the exhibit (to avoid confusion in custody cases, I usually have exhibits marked and identifies as "Mother's Exhibit #_." instead of Plaintiff's or Defendant's). You say that you move the exhibit into evidence. The opposing attorney may make an objection to the document's admission into evidence, particularly if the document hasn't been properly authenticated.

What is Hearsay?

A document or testimony may be objected to if it is hearsay. Hearsay is an out-of-court statement which is being offered in court to prove the truth of the matter asserted (in the statement). For example, if your neighbor told you that she saw your child's father drive down the street with the child unbuckled and hanging out of the car window, you could not testify that your neighbor told you that. That would be hearsay because you would be offering an out of court statement (your neighbor's statement to you about what she saw) as proof of what she said in the statement (to prove that your child's father drove down the street with the child unbuckled and hanging out of the car window). That is hearsay and is inadmissible as evidence. Your neighbor could come in and testify as to what she saw, as she is the one with firsthand knowledge and can be cross-examined about what she saw, whether she's sure it was your child's father, etc. But you cannot testify about what she said she saw. Like testimony, documents can be hearsay, which is why it is necessary to have documents properly authenticated.

An out of court statement that is not being offered to prove the truth of the statement is not hearsay. For example, if your child came home from visitation with her father and said, "Mommy is nasty," it would not be hearsay for you to testify that she said that. You are not trying to prove that you are nasty, you are simply trying to prove that your daughter said that when she returned from visitation. Because the statement ("Mommy is nasty") is not being offered to prove the truth of the matter stated (that Mommy is nasty), but is being offered for a different reason, it is not hearsay. There are a number of exceptions to the hearsay rule, but an in-depth discussion of the rules of evidence is outside the scope of this book. If you are representing yourself, it is worth your while to go to your local law library and find a book on evidence.

Once you have presented your evidence, through direct examination of your witnesses, presentation of exhibits, and cross-examination of the other side's witnesses, you will each give closing arguments. While you need to adapt your closing argument to the evidence that was presented, it is helpful to have your closing argument prepared before you go to court. Many attorneys write their closing argument first, and then plan their witnesses and exhibits around the argument to make sure that all of the information in the closing argument has been properly presented as evidence before the court. Make sure that you behave in a professional manner throughout the trial. If the judge rules against you, save your reaction until you are out of the courthouse and in your car. Likewise, if the judge rules in your favor, do not gloat. Chances are, you will be in front of the same judge and court staff again, and you do not want to be remembered as a sore loser or a gleeful winner in the eyes of the judge, clerks, or bailiffs.

6. Put yourself in the judge's place. Your judge does not have any background into your situation except for the admissible evidence presented in the court. The judge may not ever see your children and will never be as invested in them as you are. The judge is seeing you and your child's father for the first time, and he will only be able to make decisions based upon what he sees and what evidence is presented.

7. Unravel the facts. The other parent may present a story that seems very simple and easy to swallow. The truth is often far more difficult. Concise and accurate presentation of facts is crucial. Timelines, charts, graphs, videos, and other forms of demonstrative evidence which break down cumbersome amounts of information into tangible and easy-to-read exhibits can be better ways of producing evidence than lengthy testimony about facts that seem less important when taken individually. The truth is essential. If you did something that makes you appear less than perfect, explain why you did what you did. Remember, you are presenting facts, not opinions. Let the judge form the correct opinion himself, based on your presentation of the evidence.

8. Weave the facts. Fit individual facts, which seem unimportant when taken separately, into the larger context. Make sure that you take all your evidence and present it in such a way that the end result is a cohesive story that can be comprehended by someone who did not live it.

9. Poke holes in his story. Nothing can be as simple and black-and-white as his story will be. Find the holes. Dig, dig, dig in preparing the case. Find the truth, then find the admissible evidence.

10. Let your closing argument be the lightbulb over your judge's head. Highlight the very best evidence supporting why your version is the truth, and why the father's cannot be.

CHAPTER 9: The Short List – The 10 Most Important Things To Remember In Your Custody and Visitation Case

1. Bashing your child's other parent will get you nowhere. In fact, it may lose your case.
2. Be prepared to address all the child custody factors, showing why each factor supports your desired outcome.
3. Live as if you have a private investigator following you at all times.
4. Figure out how to tell your story through admissible evidence.
5. Work as a team with your attorney. Assist in gathering and organizing information.
6. Remember that guardians ad litem and court-appointed evaluators are relied upon heavily by judges. Prepare with your attorney before meeting with them.
7. Always tell the truth, but don't spill your guts. Be ready to address and explain unflattering facts.
8. Focus on the positive. Be able to show the court the unique and wonderful aspects of your parenting.
9. Come to court prepared. The more prepared you are, the less nervous you will be.
10. Your courtroom demeanor may be the most important

facet of your case. Do not make faces and do not lose your temper, no matter what.

APPENDIX

Child Support Guideline Worksheet

			Case #:	Quick Consult
Style:	Quick Consult			
Worksheet of:			Date:	

A. Gross Income of Parties

	Wife	Husband	
1. Monthly Gross Income of Each Party:	$ 4,167.00	$ 8,333.00	**Spousal Support:**
2. Spousal Support Payable between Parties:	$ 0.00	$ 0.00	**0.00**
3. Adjustment for Support of "Other" Children:	$ 0.00	$ 0.00	Spousal Support Payor:
4. Adjustment of Self-Employment Tax:	$ 0.00	$ 0.00	Husband
5. Statutory Gross Income for Support:	$ 4,167.00	$ 8,333.00	**Child Support**
6. Combined Income:	$ 12,500.00		Wife is Custodian
7. Combined Proposed Income Deviations:	**Income Shares**		Child Support Payor is:
	33.3%	66.7%	Husband
8. Number of Children: 1	Ages		

B. Child Support

1. Scheduled Amount for Basic Child Support:		$ 1,229.00	* From Support Table
2. Work-related Child Care Costs:		$ 1,000.00	
3. Medical Insurance for Child/Children:	**Wife**	**Husband**	
	$ 0.00	$ 100.00	
4. Total Child Support Need (Sum: 1+2+3+4):			**Child Support Need**
			$ 2,329.00
5. Child Support Obligation of Each Party: (Total Support Need x Income Share)	$ 776.00	$ 1,553.00	
6. Direct Payment of Medical Insurance:	$ 0.00	$ -100.00	
7. Each Party's Presumptive Guideline Share:	$ 776.00	$ 1,453.00	
8. Presumptive Guideline Support Payable by:Husband			**Guideline Child Support**
			$ 1,453.00

C. Proposed Deviations from Guideline Support

	Presumptive Guideline Support Payable by: Husband	Guideline Support
1.		$ 1,453.00
		$
	Proposed Child Support, After Deviations:	$ 1,453.00

Number of Persons in Husband 's household:
The Poverty Guideline threshold income for this number of household members is:

	Annual Income:	Monthly Income:
	$ 0.00	$ 0.00

D: Proposed Child Support Payable To Wife By Husband

Total Child Support
$ 1,453.00

Submitted by: Counsel for:

Child Custody Survival Guide

Child Support Guideline Worksheet

Style:	Quick Consult		**Case #:**	Quick Consult
Worksheet of:			**Date:**	

A. Gross Income of Parties

	Wife	**Husband**	
1. Monthly Gross Income of Each Party:	$ 4,167.00	$ 8,333.00	**Spousal Support:** **0.00** Spousal Support Payor: Husband
2. Spousal Support Payable between Parties:	$ 0.00	$ 0.00	
3. Adjustment for Support of "Other" Children:	$ 0.00	$ 0.00	
4. Adjustment of Self-Employment Tax:	$ 0.00	$ 0.00	
5. Statutory Gross Income for Support:	$ 4,167.00	$ 8,333.00	**Child Support** Wife is Custodian Child Support Payor is: Husband
6. Combined Income: $ 12,500.00			
7. Combined Proposed Income Deviations:	**Income Shares**		
	33.3%	66.7%	
8. Number of Children: 2	Ages		

B. Child Support

	Wife	**Husband**	
1. Scheduled Amount for Basic Child Support:		$ 1,823.00	* From Support Table
2. Work-related Child Care Costs:		$ 1,000.00	
3. Medical Insurance for Child/Children:	$ 0.00	$ 100.00	
4. Total Child Support Need (Sum: 1+2+3+4):			**Child Support Need** $ 2,923.00
5. Child Support Obligation of Each Party: (Total Support Need x Income Share)	$ 974.00	$ 1,949.00	
6. Direct Payment of Medical Insurance:	$ 0.00	$ -100.00	
7. Each Party's Presumptive Guideline Share:	$ 974.00	$ 1,849.00	
8. Presumptive Guideline Support Payable by: Husband			**Guideline Child Support** $ 1,849.00

C. Proposed Deviations from Guideline Support

	Presumptive Guideline Support Payable by: Husband	Guideline Support
1.		$ 1,849.00 $
	Proposed Child Support, After Deviations:	$ 1,849.00

Number of Persons in	Husband	's household:

	Annual Income:	Monthly Income:
The Poverty Guideline threshold income for this number of household members is:	$ 0.00	$ 0.00

D: Proposed Child Support Payable To Wife By Husband

Total Child Support

$ 1,849.00

Submitted by:	Counsel for:

Child Custody Survival Guide

SHARED CUSTODY SUPPORT - Shared Calculation

For support cases in which each parent has a child or children more than 90 days per year.

Style:	Quick Consult	Case #:	Quick Consult
Worksheet of:		Date:	

A. Gross Income of Parents

	Wife	Husband	Payor Spouse:
Gross Income:	$ 4,166.00	$ 8,333.00	Husband
Payment Method:	Per Month	Per Month	Spousal Payor is: Husband/Wife
Monthly Gross Income:	$ 4166	$ 8333	
2. Spousal Support Between Parties: $ 0.00	$ 0	$ 0	
3. Adjustment for Support of "Other" Children:	$ 0.00	$ 0.00	
4. Adjustment for Self Employment Tax:	$ 0.00	$ 0.00	
5. Adjusted Income for Child Support:	$ 4166	$ 8333	
6. Combined Adjusted Income: $ 12499	Income Share		
7. Each Party's Percent of Combined Income:	33.3%	66.7%	

B. Support Need of Children

Number of Children: 1   Ages:

		Husband	
1. Child Support from Guideline Table:		$ 1229	From Child Support Table
2. Total Shared Support (Guideline Table X 1.4):		$ 1721	

	Wife	Husband	Total Days:
3. Total days in year each parent has children:	275	90	365
4. Each parent's custody Share (%):	75.3%	24.7%	

C. Support Obligation of Husband

1. Basic support obligation to Wife:	$ 1296	Wife 's Custody Share (line B.4) X Total Shared Support (line B.2)
2. Work-related childcare costs of Wife:	$ 1,000.00	
3. Health Insurance paid by Wife:	$ 0.00	
4. Sum 1+2+3 = Support Subtotal for Wife:	$ 2296	
Husband 's Support Obligation Subtotal:	$ 1531	Total Support (Line C.4) X Husband 's Income Share (Line A.7)

D. Support Obligation of Wife

1. Basic support obligation to Husband:	$ 424	Husband 's Custody Share (line B.4) X Total Shared Support (line B.2)
2. Work-related childcare costs of Husband:	$ 0.00	
3. Health Insurance paid by Husband:	$ 100.00	
4. Sum 1+2+3 = Support Subtotal for Husband:	$ 524	
Wife 's Support Obligation Subtotal:	$ 175	Total Support (Line C.4) X Wife 's Income Share

E. Each Party's Support Share

Husband	Wife	Net Child Support Payable to: Wife
$ 1531	- $ 175	= $ 1356

Submitted By: Counsel For:

Child Custody Survival Guide

SHARED CUSTODY SUPPORT - Shared Calculation

For support cases in which each parent has a child or children more than 90 days per year.

Style: Quick Consult		**Case #:** Quick Consult	
Worksheet of:		**Date:**	

A. Gross Income of Parents

	Wife	**Husband**	**Payor Spouse:**
Gross Income:	$ 4,166.00	$ 8,333.00	**Husband**
Payment Method:	Per Month	Per Month	**Spousal Payor is: Husband/Wife**
Monthly Gross Income:	$ 4166	$ 8333	
2. Spousal Support Between Parties: $ 0.00	$ 0	$ 0	
3. Adjustment for Support of "Other" Children:	$ 0.00	$ 0.00	
4. Adjustment for Self Employment Tax:	$ 0.00	$ 0.00	
5. Adjusted Income for Child Support:	$ 4166	$ 8333	
6. Combined Adjusted Income: $ 12499		**Income Share**	
7. Each Party's Percent of Combined Income:	33.3%	66.7%	

B. Support Need of Children

Number of Children: 2   Ages:

1. Child Support from Guideline Table:		$ 1823	From Child Support Table
2. Total Shared Support (Guideline Table X 1.4):		$ 2552	

	Wife	**Husband**	**Total Days:**
3. Total days in year each parent has children:	275	90	365
4. Each parent's custody Share (%):	75.3%	24.7%	

C. Support Obligation of Husband

1. Basic support obligation to **Wife**:	$ 1923	**Wife** 's Custody Share (line B.4) X Total Shared Support (line B.2)
2. Work-related childcare costs of **Wife**:	$ 1,000.00	
3. Health Insurance paid by **Wife**:	$ 0.00	
4. Sum 1+2+3 = Support Subtotal for **Wife**:	$ 2923	
Husband 's Support Obligation Subtotal:	$ 1949	Total Support (Line C.4) X **Husband** 's Income Share (Line A.7)

D. Support Obligation of Wife

1. Basic support obligation to **Husband**:	$ 629	**Husband** 's Custody Share (line B.4) X Total Shared Support (line B.2)
2. Work-related childcare costs of **Husband**:	$ 0.00	
3. Health Insurance paid by **Husband**:	$ 100.00	
4. Sum 1+2+3 = Support Subtotal for **Husband**:	$ 729	
Wife 's Support Obligation Subtotal:	$ 243	Total Support (Line C.4) X **Wife** 's Income Share

E. Each Party's Support Share

Husband	**Wife**	**Net Child Support Payable to: Wife**
$ 1949	- $ 243	= $ 1706

Submitted By: **Counsel For:**

Child Custody Survival Guide

SHARED CUSTODY SUPPORT - Shared Calculation

For support cases in which each parent has a child or children more than 90 days per year.

Style:	Quick Consult		Case #:	Quick Consult
Worksheet of:			Date:	

A. Gross Income of Parents

		Wife	Husband	Payor Spouse:
	Gross Income:	$ 4,166.00	$ 8,333.00	Husband
	Payment Method:	Per Month	Per Month	Spousal Payor is: Husband/Wife
	Monthly Gross Income:	$ 4166	$ 8333	
2. Spousal Support Between Parties:	$ 0.00	$ 0	$ 0	
3. Adjustment for Support of "Other" Children:		$ 0.00	$ 0.00	
4. Adjustment for Self Employment Tax:		$ 0.00	$ 0.00	
5. Adjusted Income for Child Support:		$ 4166	$ 8333	
6. Combined Adjusted Income:	$ 12499	**Income Share**		
7. Each Party's Percent of Combined Income:		33.3%	66.7%	

B. Support Need of Children

Number of Children: 1   Ages:

		Wife	Husband	
1. Child Support from Guideline Table:			$ 1229	From Child Support Table
2. Total Shared Support (Guideline Table X 1.4):			$ 1721	

	Wife	Husband	Total Days:
3. Total days in year each parent has children:	183	182	365
4. Each parent's custody Share (%):	50.1%	49.9%	

C. Support Obligation of Husband

1. Basic support obligation to **Wife**:	$ 863	**Wife**'s Custody Share (line B.4) X Total Shared Support (line B.2)
2. Work-related childcare costs of **Wife**:	$ 1,000.00	
3. Health Insurance paid by **Wife**:	$ 0.00	
4. Sum 1+2+3 = Support Subtotal for **Wife**:	$ 1863	
Husband's Support Obligation Subtotal:	$ 1242	Total Support (Line C.4) X **Husband**'s Income Share (Line A.7)

D. Support Obligation of Wife

1. Basic support obligation to **Husband**:	$ 858	**Husband**'s Custody Share (line B.4) X Total Shared Support (line B.2)
2. Work-related childcare costs of **Husband**:	$ 0.00	
3. Health Insurance paid by **Husband**:	$ 100.00	
4. Sum 1+2+3 = Support Subtotal for **Husband**:	$ 958	
Wife's Support Obligation Subtotal:	$ 319	Total Support (Line C.4) X **Wife**'s Income Share

E. Each Party's Support Share

Husband	Wife	Net Child Support Payable to: Wife
$ 1242	- $ 319	= $ 923

Submitted By: Counsel For:

Child Custody Survival Guide

SHARED CUSTODY SUPPORT - Shared Calculation

For support cases in which each parent has a child or children more than 90 days per year.

Style: Quick Consult	**Case #:** Quick Consult	
Worksheet of:	**Date:**	

A. Gross Income of Parents

	Wife	Husband	Payor Spouse:
Gross Income:	$ 4,166.00	$ 8,333.00	**Husband**
Payment Method:	Per Month	Per Month	**Spousal Payor is:** Husband/Wife
Monthly Gross Income:	$ 4166	$ 8333	
2. Spousal Support Between Parties: $ 0.00	$ 0	$ 0	
3. Adjustment for Support of "Other" Children:	$ 0.00	$ 0.00	
4. Adjustment for Self Employment Tax:	$ 0.00	$ 0.00	
5. Adjusted Income for Child Support:	$ 4166	$ 8333	
6. Combined Adjusted Income: $ 12499	**Income Share**		
7. Each Party's Percent of Combined Income:	33.3%	66.7%	

B. Support Need of Children

Number of Children: 2   Ages:

1. Child Support from Guideline Table:		$ 1823	From Child Support Table
2. Total Shared Support (Guideline Table X 1.4):		$ 2552	

	Wife	Husband	Total Days:
3. Total days in year each parent has children:	183	182	365
4. Each parent's custody Share (%):	50.1%	49.9%	

C. Support Obligation of Husband

1. Basic support obligation to **Wife**:	$ 1280	**Wife** 's Custody Share (line B.4) X Total Shared Support (line B.2)
2. Work-related childcare costs of **Wife**:	$ 1,000.00	
3. Health Insurance paid by **Wife**:	$ 0.00	
4. Sum 1+2+3 = Support Subtotal for **Wife**:	$ 2280	
Husband 's Support Obligation Subtotal:	$ 1520	Total Support (Line C.4) X **Husband** 's Income Share (Line A.7)

D. Support Obligation of Wife

1. Basic support obligation to **Husband**:	$ 1273	**Husband** 's Custody Share (line B.4) X Total Shared Support (line B.2)
2. Work-related childcare costs of **Husband**:	$ 0.00	
3. Health Insurance paid by **Husband**:	$ 100.00	
4. Sum 1+2+3 = Support Subtotal for **Husband**:	$ 1373	
Wife 's Support Obligation Subtotal:	$ 457	Total Support (Line C.4) X **Wife** 's Income Share

E. Each Party's Support Share

Husband	Wife	Net Child Support Payable to: Wife
$ 1520	- $ 457	= $ 1062

Submitted By: **Counsel For:**